Calculating with
Lotus 1-2-3
Be an expert!

The *Be an expert!* series consists of books which enable you to teach yourself in an easy and straightforward way how to work with a computer program.

You simply follow the theory and the practical exercises and ... No trouble! It works!
This series aims at being both pleasant and educational.

Also published in this series:

- Programming with QBasic
- Word Processing with Word for Windows
- Word Processing with WordPerfect
- Designing with CorelDRAW

Else van Keulen

Calculating with
Lotus 1-2-3
Be an expert!

PRISMA

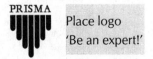

Place logo
'Be an expert!'

Prisma *Be an expert!* first published in Great Britain by

Het Spectrum
P.O. Box 2996
London N5 2TA London

Translation: George Hall
Illustrations: Jurjen Tjallema
Production: LINE UP text productions

For the English translation
© 1994 Uitgeverij Het Spectrum B.V., Utrecht

ISBN 1 85365 361 6

British Library Cataloguing-in-Publication Data.
A catalogue record for this book is available from the British Library.

Contents

Introduction

As you probably know, there are different kinds of computer programs. These programs enable you to get the computer to do the things you want. Of course, it doesn't just work by itself; you have to know how to handle computer programs and you will have to perform all sorts of actions yourself too. Good computer programs make it easy for you to work with the computer.

There are, for instance, programs for the creation and layout of text (*word processing programs*), programs for drawing and making pictures (*graphic programs*) and of course computer games. There are many different kinds of computer programs. One of these is the *spreadsheet program*.

Perhaps you have already worked with this kind of program. There are many variations. One of these is *Lotus 1-2-3*.

What can you do with a spreadsheet program?

The word 'spreadsheet' program probably doesn't mean much to you. Things may become clearer if we use a different word which is also often used instead: 'electronic worksheet'.

In bygone days, there were also devices to help calculation, such as the pen and paper, the abacus, the slide rule and (since the seventies) the pocket calculator. But the spreadsheet makes it all much easier.

The spreadsheet program is really meant for making calculations, but you can also type normal text to make headings or describe the figures. Of course, you cannot do as many things with the text as in a word processing program, but nevertheless the text can be made very attractive.

What kind of program is Lotus 1-2-3?

Lotus 1-2-3 is the most well-known and most widely sold spreadsheet program. The program enables you to work with figures quickly and easily. Lotus 1-2-3 contains a great number of functions or features which make sure the calculations are properly done and which help eliminate mistakes.

For example, you don't need to add up any numbers. If you inform Lotus 1-2-3 where the numbers are which are to be added up, the program will do it for you. And another very handy feature is that if you then change one of the numbers which were added up, Lotus 1-2-3 will adjust the total automatically.

When you have organised your figures correctly, Lotus 1-2-3 can create a diagram of these and also print the diagram on paper. This can lead to impressive results.

A special part of Lotus 1-2-3, called WYSIWYG, enables you to make attractive designs for your texts and diagrams.

Lotus 1-2-3 is a spreadsheet program, but you can also use it to manage a simple database. This is a kind of filing cabinet full of information. For instance, you could store the names and addresses of all your friends and acquaintances here.

Lotus 1-2-3 is a DOS application program. This means that you can work with it on a normal PC and that you do not need Windows to be able to run the program.

What are you going to do with Lotus 1-2-3?

Lotus 1-2-3 is a spreadsheet program, therefore you will be working with numbers a lot in this book. But we shall also let you see how to get the best out of the design and layout features when working with numbers and text. Here is a brief summary of what to expect in this book:

- keeping track of income and expenditure
- noting and working out school report marks
- sorting information
- making diagrams for bicycling speeds
- creating attractive worksheets and diagrams
- printing worksheets and diagrams
- creating macros to carry out commands quicker.

1 Whatever happened to my pocket money?

In this chapter, you will make a worksheet for keeping track of your income and expenditure. You will first start up Lotus 1-2-3 and examine what appears on the screen. You will learn how to type the information properly and how to save the worksheet.

Starting up Lotus 1-2-3

In order to work with Lotus 1-2-3, you have to start it up first.

When you switch on the computer, the *DOS prompt* appears on the screen. It looks like this:

```
c:\>
```

Behind this prompt is a flashing block or stripe. This is the *cursor*. It is waiting on input from you.

Programs are not just stored in a heap in the computer; they are stored in their own **directories**. You could compare this to a supermarket for example, where similar types of goods are placed together in their own section. Normally the Lotus 1-2-3 program will be stored in the **123R24** directory and you will have to tell the computer to go to this directory to find the Lotus 1-2-3 program (see Appendix A for more information). Therefore type:

```
cd 123r24
```

which means Change Directory and go to the directory called 123R24. Now press **Enter** (also called **Return** on some keyboards).

The following will appear on the screen:

```
C:\123R24>
```

To start up Lotus 1-2-3, type:

```
123
```

and press **Enter**.

The Lotus 1-2-3 opening screen appears.

If nothing happens and the message appears:

```
Bad command or file name
```

this means that the computer cannot find the program in the directory you typed. If you have not made a typing error, the best thing to do is to ask a parent, a friend, a teacher (or someone else who is familiar with the computer) if Lotus 1-2-3 has been correctly installed and if so, in which directory.

We shall presume that everything has gone smoothly and Lotus 1-2-3 has started up correctly.

The Lotus 1-2-3 screen

When you have started up the program, the opening screen appears.

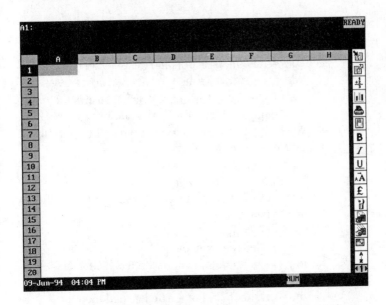

This screen probably doesn't mean much to you. It is almost completely empty.

Because Lotus 1-2-3 is a spreadsheet program which is used to calculate numbers, there have to be boxes to put these numbers in. We call these boxes *cells*. The cells are all numbered. There are letters along the top of the screen, from A to H. These are the letters which indicate the *columns*. At the left-hand side of the screen there are numbers, from 1 to 20. These numbers indicate the *rows* of the spreadsheet.

You can define which cell you want by naming the column letter and row number. Now you will understand the text in the top left-hand corner of the screen. This shows the cell in which the cursor is situated at this moment. We also refer to this as the *cell address.* Press one of the cursor keys on your computer. You will see that the cursor moves in the corresponding direction and the relevant cell address is shown in the top left-hand corner. We call this the currently *active* cell, because if you now type data (information) such as numbers or text, it will be placed in this cell. As you see, the currently active cell is A1 at this moment.

When working in the worksheet we shall use the term *cell pointer* because this always indicates the cell to be used.

The whole area containing all these boxes in which you can enter data is called the *worksheet*. In fact, what you see on your screen is only a small part of the worksheet. Press the **End** key and then the Cursor Down key. The cell pointer is now located in cell A8192, thus in row 8192 of column A. Now press **End** again and then the Cursor Right key. The cell pointer is now in the cell with the address IV8192, thus in row 8192 of column IV. This is the very last cell in the worksheet. If you wish to return to the first cell quickly, press **Home**.

You have now learned to use a number of keys for moving through the worksheet. We have made a list of these below for convenience:

key	effect
←	cell one cell to the left
→	cell pointer one cell to the right
↑	cell pointer one cell up
↓	cell pointer one cell down

Home   to cell A1
PgUp   one screen upwards
PgDn   one screen downwards
Ctrl+←   one screen leftwards
Ctrl+→   one screen rightwards

End, →   to the last column
End, ↓   to the last row

The **F5** key has a special function. If you press it, Lotus 1-2-3 will ask for the address to which you want to go. You can now type the address of the cell in question. Then press **Enter**. The cell pointer goes immediately to that cell which is very convenient if the cell is far away from your present position. We refer to this key as the GOTO key.

Try out all these keys and keep in mind that you can
always return to the beginning by pressing **Home**.

Working with the menus

Perhaps you have worked with other computer programs. If so, you may be wondering why there is no
menu bar. In other programs, there is almost always
a menu bar along the top of the screen. The Lotus
1-2-3 opening screen is a bit bare.

However, Lotus 1-2-3 does have a menu bar but it
has been hidden. If you press the / key (called the
slash key, mostly at the lower right-hand corner of
the keyboard next to Shift), you might get a sur-
prise. Two rows suddenly appear at the top of the
screen. The top line is the main menu. The second

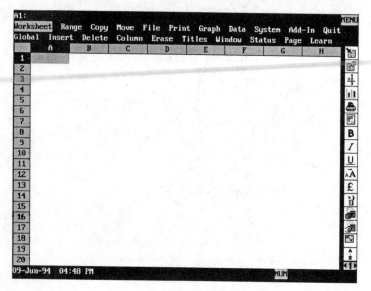

line shows the options which are available 'under' the marked command in the top line. If there are no further options available for a command in the top line, the second line will give a short description of the marked command.

You choose a command from the menu by placing the cursor on it and pressing **Enter** or by typing the first letter of the required command. You can leave the menu by pressing the **Esc** key.

Practice this by pressing the / key to activate the menu bar. Select **Range** from the menu by pressing **R** or by moving the cursor to the command and pressing **Enter**. You will now see a list of all the options which are available in the **Range** menu. Select **Format** by pressing **Enter** (the cell pointer was already situated on this option). Then move the cursor to **General** by pressing the Cursor Right key. You will see that the second line gives a description of the available options as you move rightwards. Don't press **Enter** this time, press the **Esc** key three times. Each time you press **Esc** you move a level upwards, back towards the 'surface' as it were. You now return to the worksheet, the menu bar has disappeared and nothing has changed in the worksheet.

Working with the SmartIcons

At the far right of your screen there is a bar with icons, which are small pictures or symbols which represent functions in the Lotus 1-2-3 program. If you have a mouse, you can use these icons to

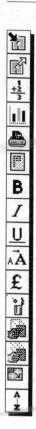

quickly activate the functions which are often used.
In that case, you do not need to first open the menu
bar to choose the required command(s); you can
just directly click on an icon to execute a command.
These icons are called *SmartIcons*.

If you want to know what a particular icon does,
place the mouse pointer on it and press the **right**
mouse button. A short description of the workings
of the icon is given above the worksheet as long as
you hold down the right mouse button. The description disappears as soon as you release the mouse
button.

Place the mouse pointer on the top icon and press
the right mouse button. The description 'Saves the
current worksheet file to a disk' appears.

If you click on the bottom icon with the **left** mouse
button, a different set of icons appears. There are in
total 66 icons, divided into 7 sets. The number
shown in the bottom icon indicates with which set
you are working. In this book, we shall generally
work with the menu bar, but in cases where it is
much easier to use the SmartIcons we shall say so.
Working with the menu bar does however give
more insight into the workings of Lotus 1-2-3, and if
you do not have a mouse, you can still execute all
the commands.

Statements

At the top right-hand corner of the opening screen
you will see the text 'READY'. This indicates the

mode in which Lotus 1-2-3 is working, in other words, the current situation of the program. Statements may also be shown in the bottom right-hand corner of the screen.

The statement 'READY' means that Lotus 1-2-3 is ready to accept data from the user. We shall give a list below of the most frequently-shown statements, along with their significance. Other statements will be discussed at the relevant places in this book.

mode indicator	meaning
READY	This statement is shown in the top right-hand corner when Lotus 1-2-3 is ready to accept data from the user.
EDIT	You have pressed **F2** and you can now change the contents of a cell if you wish. As soon as you press **Enter**, the statement will become READY again.
ERROR	This is a very important message. If you want to know what has gone wrong, press **F1**. A help screen appears containing information about the error.
HELP	A help screen is being shown. You can return to the worksheet by pressing **Esc**.
LABEL	You are entering data in a cell and Lotus 1-2-3 recognizes that this is text input.
MENU	You have pressed the / key so that the menu bar is being displayed.

POINT   Lotus 1-2-3 is expecting you to
                 define a range of cells.

VALUE   You are entering data in a cell and
                 Lotus 1-2-3 has recognized that this
                 is numerical input.

WAIT   Lotus 1-2-3 is busy carrying out a
                 command. You will have to wait
                 until READY appears on the screen
                 once more.

The statements shown at the bottom of the screen
are called *status indicators*. The most important of
these are:

status indicator   meaning

CAPS   You have pressed the **CapsLock**
                 key.

CIRC   You have entered a formula which
                 refers to itself.

END   You have pressed the **End** key.
                 Lotus 1-2-3 expects you to press one
                 of the cursor keys.

NUM   You have pressed the **NumLock**
                 key.

OVR   You have pressed the **Insert** key,
                 which means that you have activat-
                 ed the *overwrite* mode. New data
                 are not added to the old ones, they
                 are written over the old ones.

CALC   Lotus 1-2-3 has to calculate the for-
                 mulas in the worksheet.

SCROLL   The **ScrollLock** key has been
                 pressed.

Balancing the budget

Entering text

After all this theory it's time we got down to actually doing something.

We shall create a worksheet in which you can place all your income and expenditure side by side.

☞ Press the **Home** key to place the cell pointer in cell A1.
☞ Now type:

```
Income and expenditure in June
```

You will see that the text first appears at the top of the screen. If you make a typing mistake, press **Backspace** to remove the mistake and then type the correct letter.

☞ Press **Enter**.

The typed text is now placed in the worksheet.

☞ Press the ↓ key twice so that the cell pointer is positioned in cell A3.
☞ Type:

```
income
```

☞ Now press the → key twice to move the cell pointer to cell C3.

☞ Type:

```
expenditure
```

Now you have to specify the income and expenditure underneath these headings. We give an example here, but you will have your own categories so you can enter them instead if you want.

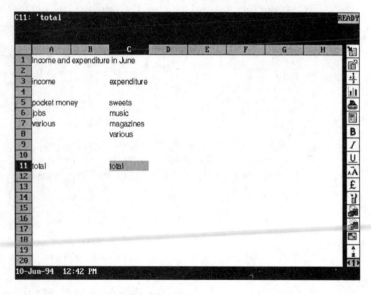

Make sure to leave space for the total.

Making the columns wider

Some of the headings are wider than the columns in which they have been placed. Because the column next-door is empty, that doesn't matter too much. But when we want to enter figures into these columns, we will have to do something about it.

☞ Place the cell pointer somewhere in column A.
☞ Open the menu bar by pressing the / key.
☞ Select the **Worksheet** command and press **Enter**.

You want to change the column width, so move the cursor to the Column option.

☞ Choose **Column** by moving the cursor to it and pressing **Enter**.

The cursor is now positioned on the **Set-Width** option and the description 'Specify width for current column' is given. This is exactly what we need.

☞ Press **Enter**.
☞ Type '12'.

This is enough for our list. You can enter any number between 1 and 240.

When you press **Enter**, the first column becomes wide enough to take 12 characters. This is shown between the square brackets at the top: [W12]. This indicates that you are no longer using the standard Lotus 1-2-3 settings, you have changed the column width to 12 yourself.

☞ Do the same for column C.

Entering the numbers

The worksheet layout is now ready. You can now begin to add the numbers in column B and column

D. Enter the amount of pocket money you get each month behind 'pocket money'.

Changing the numbers style

You have entered ordinary numbers for each category but if we want, we can fill in real financial amounts.

☞ Position the cell pointer in cell B5.
☞ Press the / key to open the menu bar.
☞ Select **Range** and press **Enter**. Now select **Format** and press **Enter**.

A list of options appears from which you can choose a required style or format. You can apply this format to a whole range.

☞ Select **Currency** by moving the cursor and then press **Enter**.

You now have to choose the number of decimals to be shown in the figures, in other words, the number of figures behind the point. Of course, we wish to show pounds and pence so we want two figures behind the point. Lotus 1-2-3 already suggests 2. Accept this proposal by simply pressing **Enter**.

Then you have to specify the range to which this format should apply. This is the entire area in which you want to enter numbers. The first cell is already indicated, B5.

☞ Now use the ↓ key to move downwards to cell B11, or even lower if you have created more rows for income and expenditure than we have.

☞ Then press **Enter**.

All the amounts which you have entered in this column have now been changed to financial amounts. A sterling sign has been added and there are two decimal places behind the point.

☞ Do the same for the range D5 to D11.

 You can also use the **Currency format** icon to format a range of cells to a financial layout. In that case, you first have to mark the range and then click on the icon. You mark the range by positioning the mouse pointer on the first cell of the required range, pressing and holding down the left mouse button and dragging the mouse pointer over the range of cells. The selected range is shown in a different colour or shading on the screen. When you have selected the required range, release the mouse button and click on the icon using the left mouse button.

Whichever way you have selected the ranges, the worksheet should now look like this:

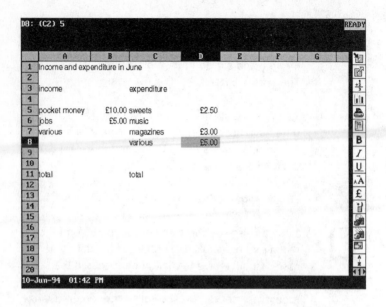

Selecting ranges

In the previous section you selected a range by placing the cell pointer on the first cell of the required range and then marking the range by pressing the cursor keys. You did this prior to choosing the command. But you can also select a range in a different way.

If you have to select a range while you are busy with a command, and the first cell has already been correctly named by Lotus 1-2-3, then press the point or full-stop key (.) twice and type the cell address of the last cell in the range. Then press **Enter**.

If the correct cells are not shown, type the cell address of the first cell, then two dots (..) and type the address of the last cell in the range. Then press

Enter.

In principle, we shall not give further instructions about how to select cells. Choose the method you yourself prefer.

Working with functions

The cells behind the totals have not yet been filled in. The amounts listed above should be added up and entered in these cells. But you don't need to do this yourself! Lotus 1-2-3 has *functions* for doing this kind of work.

Each function in Lotus 1-2-3 begins with an *at* sign (@). In this way, Lotus 1-2-3 can recognize that you want to use a function and not a normal text. Then

you have to enter the name of the function, such as
SUM for instance, for adding up figures. Behind
SUM you have to enter between brackets the so-
called *arguments*, which are the values which the
function has to deal with. In this case, the arguments for the SUM function are the cells which
have to be added up.

The SUM function is carried out as follows:

☞ Place the cell pointer in B11.
☞ Type the following:

```
@SUM(B5..B9)
```

☞ Then press **Enter**.

As soon as you have pressed **Enter**, the numbers in
cells B5 to B9 are added up and displayed in cell
B11. The input line at the top of the screen shows
the formula you have used. In fact, the two dots
actually mean *up to and including*.

Cell D11 should display the sum of the cells D5 to
D9.

☞ Therefore, type in D11:

```
@SUM(D5..D9)
```

An excellent feature of this function is that the result
is automatically altered when you change a value in
one of the cells in the selected ranges.

To see how much money you have left at the end
of the month, you have to subtract the total expenditure from the total income. We shall not use a
function for this, we shall simply subtract the contents of one cell from the contents of the other. This
is quite normal in Lotus 1-2-3.

☞ In cell E11 type the text 'balance'.

Then give cell F11 the Currency format:

☞ Press the / key.
☞ Select **Range**.
☞ Select **Format**.
☞ Select **Currency**.
☞ Press the **Enter** key twice.
☞ Now enter:

```
+B11-D11
```

☞ Press the **Enter** key.

By placing a plus in front of B11, you indicate that
you do not want to enter a text, you want to enter a
cell address. If you do not do this, Lotus 1-2-3 will
assume that you are entering normal text and no
calculation will take place; the input will be placed
as text in the cell.

Other calculation functions

Up until now, you have worked with the @SUM()
function. But there are many more that you can use
for calculation. Here is a list of functions which you
will often use:

function	significance
@ROUND()	The @ROUND() function is used to round off a number to a specified number of decimals. We shall deal with this in more detail in chapter 2.
@AVG()	The @AVG() function is used to calculate the average of a number of values. We shall also deal with this function in more detail in chapter 2.
@MAX()	The @MAX() function calculates the highest value in a selected range of cells.
@MIN()	The @MIN() function calculates the smallest value in a selected range of cells.
@NOW	The @NOW function adds the current date to the worksheet. We shall give an example of this in chapter 3.
@RAND	The @RAND function places a random number on the screen. This function is useful if you need random numbers for a game or a lottery for instance. We shall give an example of this in the last chapter.

Copying data

Now that you have entered all the income and expenditure for June, you can make a worksheet for July. You don't need to begin all over again. This is one of the great benefits of working with a spreadsheet program.

Copying cells

In order to copy the whole block of data, place the
cell pointer in cell A1 (press **Home**).

☞ Then activate the menu by pressing the / key.

The third command on the menu bar is **Copy**. This
is what we need to copy the data. That is also
shown when you place the cursor on this option;
on the second line, a description is given: 'Copy a
cell or range of cells'.

☞ Therefore move the cursor to **Copy** and press **Enter**.

Now you have to define what you want to copy. In
our example, that is all the cells between A1 and
F11.

You can simply type A1..F11, but you can also mark
the required area using the cursor keys. Press the →
key five times so that the first row from A to F is
marked. Now press the ↓ key ten times so that the
cell pointer is now situated in cell F11 and the entire
area from A1 to F11 is marked. Now press **Enter**.
You can also drag the mouse across this area to
mark it.

The marking disappears and the question 'To
where?' appears. Now you have to specify the area
to which you want to copy the data. Do not place
the copy directly under the first block; leave a
couple of rows empty, that makes it all a bit clearer.
Use the ↓ key to go to cell A14 and press the **Enter**
key. A copy of the whole block now appears, start-
ing at cell A14.

Caution: If some information had already been placed at that position, Lotus 1-2-3 would just over-write it and the old information is thus lost. So you will have to pay attention.

Lotus 1-2-3 is rather clever. Go to cell B24 using the cursor keys. At that position there is a copy of the first SUM function. But Lotus 1-2-3 has already made adjustments to the arguments in the function. Now the cells B5 to B9 are not added up; the cells B18 to B22 are added up instead. Quite bright, don't you think? Lotus 1-2-3 has also copied the lay-out such as the currency symbols and the number of decimals.

You don't have to do much to complete the second block.

Changing the cell contents

You now have two examples of the data for June in your worksheet. This is not our intention. We shall have to adjust the second block.

☞ Place the cell pointer at cell A14.
☞ Press the **F2** key.

This is the EDIT key. That is also shown in the top right-hand corner of the screen. This indicates that the cell contents can now be altered.

The cursor is now flashing in the input line at the top of the screen. We wish to alter the month of June to July.

☞ Press the **Backspace** key until 'June' has disappeared.

☞ Now type:

```
July
```

☞ Press the **Enter** key.

The new text is adopted into the worksheet.

If you want to adjust the amounts for the items in July, you do not first have to press the **F2** key. Just place the cell pointer at the required cell and type the relevant amount. Then press **Enter**. The new amount is adopted immediately.

Because Lotus 1-2-3 has already adjusted the functions automatically and has placed the proper cells in the arguments, the program is able to calculate the new totals as soon as you enter a new amount in one of the cells for July.

Saving the file

Now that you have created this impressive list, it is time to save the worksheet. If you just stopped and switched off the computer, you would lose all your work and that is not our intention.

The worksheet has to be saved in a file. (If you don't know much about files and directories, read Appendix A first.) The worksheet is saved as follows:

☞ Open the menu bar by pressing the / key.
☞ Select **File** by moving the cursor to it and pressing **Enter**.
☞ Select **Save**.
☞ Type a name for the worksheet (max. 8 letters or numbers or a combination of these), for instance·

CASH

☞ Press **Enter**.

Closing down Lotus

When you have had enough, you have to close Lotus 1-2-3 down in an orderly way. Never just switch the computer off, even if you don't want to save your worksheet!

Close Lotus 1-2-3 down as follows:

☞ Open the menu bar by pressing the / key.
☞ Select **Quit**.
☞ Select **Yes**.

Lotus 1-2-3 is ended and the DOS prompt appears on the screen.

What have you learned in this chapter?

You have learned a number of basic skills in this first chapter. We shall list them here:

- entering text
- entering numbers
- using functions
- copying cells
- altering data
- saving the worksheet
- closing down Lotus 1-2-3.

Ideas and suggestions

By applying everything you have learned in this chapter, you can do much more than creating this worksheet alone. You can extend it to cover the whole year, you can do the book-keeping for the entire household or the local amateur football club or the swimming club or whatever.

2 Working out your school report figures

Of course you can put Lotus 1-2-3 to many more uses than only calculating income and expenditure. For instance, you can create a list of all your written and oral exams so that Lotus 1-2-3 can calculate what your final school report figures will be. If your school doesn't work with a system like this, you can use the same kind of list to allocate marks to the players in your favourite football team to assess their performance, or to keep track of the scores in the Open Golf championship or to judge the Eurovision Song contest at home.

Your head may be spinning at the end of this chapter due to all the information supplied. For this reason we shall also outline how to work with the Lotus 1-2-3 help function so that if you get stuck somewhere, the solution to the problem can be provided.

Preparing the worksheet

Starting a new worksheet

If you still have the previous worksheet on the screen and you want to begin a new worksheet, you should first save the old one if you want to save the data. How this is done is indicated at the end of chapter 1.

When you have saved your work do not quit Lotus 1-2-3. A new worksheet is opened as follows:

☞ Press the / key to open the menu bar.
☞ Select **Worksheet**.
☞ Select **Erase**.
☞ Select **Yes**.

If you have not saved your work, Lotus 1-2-3 will ask for confirmation of your command. This is to prevent unintentional loss of data.

The computer memory is cleared, but data which have been saved are not lost. They are stored on disk. A new worksheet with the default settings is started up.

Changing the standard column width

When dealing with report figures, the greater part of the worksheet will be filled with numbers. In that case, the columns are in fact much too wide. If you enter numbers into the current worksheet, only a few of them will actually be shown on the screen and a lot of space will remain unused.

Make the columns four characters wide, beginning at column B. The quickest way of doing this is to change the standard width of the columns in the worksheet and then to make column A a little wider again.

To do this, proceed as follows:

☞ Open the menu bar by pressing the / key.
☞ Select **Worksheet**.
☞ Select **Global**.
☞ Select **Column-Width**.
☞ Type the number 4 behind 'Enter global column width (1..240):'
☞ Press **Enter**.

Now all the columns are only four characters wide. This is sufficient to enter figures consisting of maximum three numbers. But the column in which the names of the subjects are to be placed is too narrow. We shall have to widen it:

☞ Place the cell pointer anywhere in column A.
☞ Open the menu bar by pressing the / key.
☞ Select **Worksheet**.
☞ Select **Column**.
☞ Select **Set-Width**.
☞ Type the number 12 behind 'Enter column width (1..240):'
☞ Press **Enter**.

Column A is now 12 characters wide and the other columns are 4 characters wide.

The worksheet now looks like this:

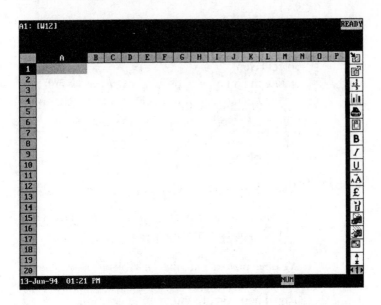

Note

When working with a worksheet, it may happen that you enter more numbers in a column than the column can accept. In that case asterisks will be shown instead of numbers.

This may be because you have not made the columns wide enough for your requirements in which case you will have to adjust the width of the column(s) in question as indicated above.

It may also be because using a function provides an answer with many decimal places which Lotus 1-2-3 attempts to show. Do not panic! The answer is not lost. You will have to adjust the format of the numbers instead of the width of the columns. This is done as follows:

☞ Place the cell pointer in the relevant cell.
☞ Press the / key to open the menu bar.

☞ Select **Range**.
☞ Select **Format**.
☞ Select **Fixed**.
☞ Define the number of decimal places you want.
☞ Define the range in your worksheet to which this
   format is to apply.
☞ Press **Enter**.

Entering text

You first have to do a lot of typework to fill in all the
subjects you take at school.

We have placed a number of subjects below. Skip
those you don't take. If you take others not displayed here, simply add them to your list.

Subject	Written Exams	Oral Exams	Average (Report %)
English			
French			
German			
Economics			
History			
Geography			
Mathematics			
Biology			
Music			
Technical			
Health Care			
Art			
Handwork			
Design			

Religious Ed.
Latin
Social Std.

Did something strange happen when you entered the text '(Report %)'? If you type a bracket, Lotus 1-2-3 thinks that you are about to type a formula, not a text.

Therefore, you have to inform Lotus 1-2-3 that you want to enter a text. This is done by typing an apostrophe (') in front of the bracket.

Lotus 1-2-3 also recognizes other signs which you enter in order to adapt the text in a cell. This is discussed further in chapter 3.

Enter in your list the subjects you take at school.

In general written exams are more important than oral. Therefore we shall count the value of these examinations in slightly different ways.

When you have entered everything as required, the screen will look something like this.

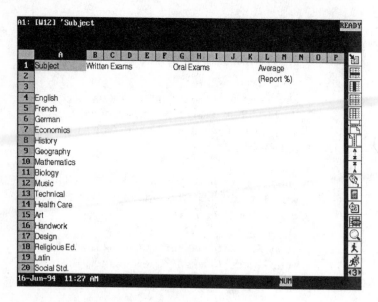

Entering the formulas

The text is now completed. Now we have to fill in
the formulas which will calculate the average of
your exams so that you can work out what your
report figures are going to be.

We shall presume that you have three written and
three oral exams each school year. Teachers who
exceed this are pure sadists.

We shall arrange it so that written exams are twice
as important as oral exams. If your school works in a
different way, change the formula to fit.

Summarising:

- Three written exams each year - this means that columns B, C and D are used for the results. The average of these will be calculated and will be counted twice in the final report.
- Three oral exams each year - columns G, H and I will be used for these results. The average of these will be counted once in the final report.
- The final report, Average (Report %) is placed in column L.

Because the result, the Average (Report %) is placed in column L, this means that the formula which calculates the average will also have to be placed in this column.

The function which calculates averages is called **@AVG()**. This is not difficult to remember. The addresses of the cells which are to be averaged are placed between the brackets. If you wanted to allow the written exams and the oral exams to be equally important, applying the function would be not at all difficult - the average for English in cell L4 would be the average of the values in the cells B4 to I4, in the same way as you did for the SUM function in chapter 1.

The present example is a bit more complicated and requires some mathematical insight. How do you calculate the average of a range in which you have to count the first part twice? The following formula is the answer. Take a close look at it. Then we shall explain it.

```
(2*@AVG(B4..D4)+@AVG(G4..I4))/3
```

First you have to calculate the average of the written exams. The formula is @AVG(B4..D4). Then you multiply this average by 2 because this result is to be counted twice. Now you have to take the average of the Oral exams. The formula for this is @AVG(G4..I4). This is added to the first part of our formula. Finally, because you have three percentages added together, divide the result by 3. This is why the formula is enclosed by brackets to let Lotus 1-2-3 know that the complete formula has to be divided by 3 and not just the last part.

The steps are as follows:

☞ Place the cell pointer on cell L4.
☞ Enter the following formula:

```
(2*@AVG(B4..D4)+@AVG(G4..I4))/3
```

When entering formulas, you have to pay very close attention to brackets and other special characters.

☞ Press **Enter**.

But ... something strange happens. The word ERR (for Error) is shown in cell L4. This is quite logical of course, since no figures have been entered with which Lotus 1-2-3 can work.

As soon as you enter a figure for a written exam, the word 'ERR' will disappear and the average will be displayed in column L. Try it out.

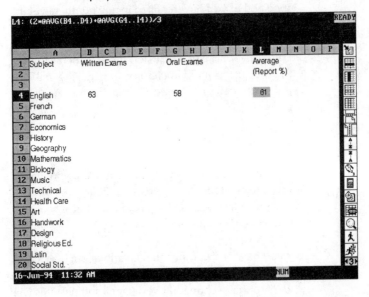

We have now filled in the formula for English but there is still a whole list of subjects for which you want to calculate the average. The easiest way of doing this is to copy the formula in cell L4 instead of

having to type the formula in all the other cells.
Therefore copy the formula in L4 to the cells below:

☞ Place the cell pointer in cell L4.
☞ Press the / key to open the menu bar.
☞ Select **Copy**.
☞ Press **Enter**, the relevant cell is already shown on
the input line at the top.
☞ Specify the range L5..L20 behind the question 'To
where?'.
☞ Press **Enter**.

Now the word 'ERR' is shown in all the cells you
specified (if you haven't filled in any numbers yet in
the corresponding rows).

Lotus 1-2-3 has again adjusted the arguments in the
formula just as it did in chapter 1. Move the cell
pointer to cell L12. The top line of the screen displays:

```
(2*@AVG(B12..D12)+@AVG(G12..I12))/3
```

As you see, Lotus 1-2-3 has assumed that you wanted to calculate the average of the figures in row 12
and place the result in L12. And that is true, that's
just what we wanted.

If you have made other specifications, such as alterations to the standard (also called *default*) column
width or have changed the decimal settings, this will
also be shown on this line at the top of the screen.

Saving the worksheet

The layout is completed. Save the worksheet before entering the exam results.

☞ Press the / key to open the menu bar.
☞ Select **File**.
☞ Select **Save**.
☞ Type a name for the worksheet:

REPORT

☞ Press **Enter**.

You then return to the worksheet and you can begin to enter the exam figures. The worksheet is stored as a file on disk.

If you like, you can now close down Lotus 1-2-3 without the data being lost.

It is advisable to save the worksheet each time you have entered a reasonable amount of data.

Saving an existing file

Saving a file which already has a name takes place a little differently than saving a file for the first time.

Imagine that you have entered numbers in several rows and you want to save the file before continuing. In this way, you know that if anything unexpected happens (a power cut, the telephone rings and your brother pulls out the plug while you are away, your mother spills tea on the keyboard...) the information will be safe. Proceed as follows:

☞ Press.the / key to open the menu bar.
☞ Select **File**.
☞ Select **Save**.

Lotus 1-2-3 suggests the same name as you already gave to the file. This is fine because there is no need to give the file a different name.

☞ Press **Enter**.

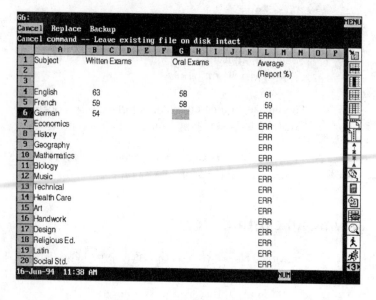

You will see that three options are provided:

Cancel   If you choose **Cancel**, the Save command will not be carried out and nothing else will happen. Any changes are not written to disk, they only exist in working memory.

Replace   If you choose **Replace**, the new version of the worksheet is written over the old one on disk.

Backup   If you choose **Backup**, the old version of the worksheet is stored with the extension BAK and the new version is stored under the normal file name along with the normal extension WK1. If anything should go wrong by any chance, you then have the previous version to fall back on.

Normally you would choose **Replace**.

☞ Select **Replace**.
☞ Press **Enter**.

The file is now stored on disk and you can continue working or close down Lotus 1-2-3 if you prefer.

 Clicking on the **Save** icon with the mouse also enables you to save an existing file quickly and easily.

Retrieving a file

Imagine that you have closed Lotus 1-2-3 and you want to work with the REPORT file. You now have to *Retrieve* it. This is done as follows:

☞ Start up Lotus 1-2-3 if necessary.
☞ Press the / key to open the menu bar.
☞ Select **File**.
☞ Select **Retrieve**.
☞ Type the name of the required file:

REPORT

☞ Press **Enter**.

The worksheet is now displayed on the screen.

Instead of carrying out the last step, typing the name of the file, you can also press the cursor keys to move through the names of the files shown at the top of the screen. The names of all the files in the current directory are shown here. When you reach REPORT.WK1, press the **Enter** key. The worksheet appears on the screen.

 The **Retrieve** icon also enables you to open an existing file easily and quickly.

The extension WK1 behind the name is added automatically by Lotus 1-2-3. This indicates the type of file we are dealing with, in this case a worksheet from Lotus 1-2-3.

Giving a name to a range

In principle, the REPORT worksheet is completed and you only need to add the figures. But because your parent(s) have promised you a new bike or saxophone lessons or a disco birthday party if your average is high enough, you want to work out the average of all your marks. This means working out the average of the average.

This is very easy and we shall also indicate another convenient feature of Lotus 1-2-3 at the same time.

First enter the formula for the average of the averages:

☞ Go to cell L22.
☞ Type the following formula:

```
@AVG(L4..L20)
```

If you have filled in marks throughout the report, the average of the average will now be shown in cell L22, otherwise the word 'ERR' is shown. This is no disaster as you already know.

But how often have you made an error when typing cell addresses? Wouldn't it be handier to have another means of telling Lotus 1-2-3 which range of cells should be used?

Fortunately, this method does exist. This method uses *range names*. You only need to tell Lotus 1-2-3 that a certain range has a certain name and in all further actions you only need to use this name to refer to this range of cells regardless of the function being used.

To illustrate this, we shall use the previous formula. We worked out the average of the range L4 to L20. We shall now assign a name to this range.

☞ Place the cell pointer in cell L4.
☞ Press the / key to display the menu bar on the screen.
☞ Select **Range**.
☞ Select **Name**.
☞ Select **Create**.

☞ Type the name you want to give to the range, for example:

AVERAGE

☞ Press **Enter**.
☞ Define the range to which you want to give this name L4..L20.
☞ Press **Enter**.

You have now given the name 'AVERAGE' to this range.

Now place the cell pointer at cell L22. See what has happened? The top line of the screen shows that Lotus 1-2-3 has replaced the cell addresses by the name you have just given to the range.

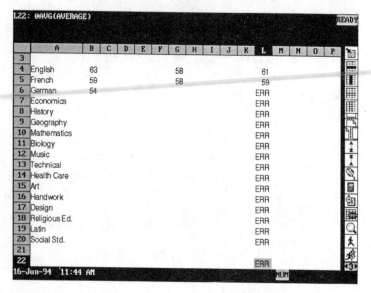

If you want to execute a different function with this range, for instance, adding all the averages up, you do not need to specify the cell addresses anymore, you only need to give the name of the range, 'AVERAGE'. Easy isn't it?

When working with range names, it is advisable to use clear and meaningful names. Do not use lengthy names, this only increases the chance of typing errors. Lotus 1-2-3 cannot handle names longer than 15 characters.

Also pay attention to the following rules when using range names:

- A name must always begin with a letter.
- You must not use spaces or hyphens in a name.
- You can also use numbers, dots and underlining characters in a name.

Help!!!

After practising a couple of times, you will realise that Lotus 1-2-3 can do a lot and has many commands and functions available. It's impossible to explain them all within the scope of this book. We can only give an outline of the basic skills and hope that you are interested enough to continue and to use these basic skills in your own personal worksheets.

But you are not completely alone. Lotus 1-2-3 can help you by means of its extensive help function.

You can make use of this help function in different ways:

- general
- dealing with a certain topic (so-called *context-oriented*).

You can activate the general help function by pressing the **F1** key without having selected a command. A dialog window with the name '1-2-3 Main Help Index' appears on the screen.

This main index contains a lengthy alphabetical list of topics about which you can ask for information. You can move down through the list by pressing the cursor keys, but you can do this quicker by clicking with the mouse on the arrows at the right-hand side of the list.

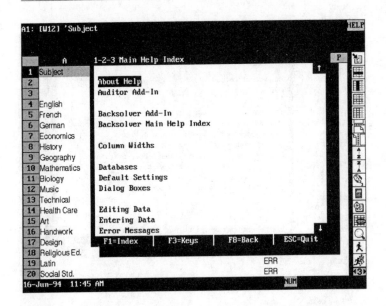

 You can also click on the icon with the **question mark** (icon set 4) to activate the general help function.

Imagine you have forgotten how to change the column width. In order to find out how this is done, proceed as follows:

☞ Press **F1**.
☞ Use the cursor keys to move down through the list until you reach 'Column Widths'.
☞ Press **Enter**.

A help screen now appears with information about setting column widths.

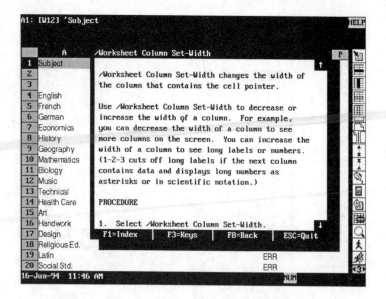

When you want to return to the worksheet, press the **Esc** key. If you want to return to the main index, press **F8**. You can then select another topic about which you want to obtain information.

The second way of requesting help is *context-oriented*. This is a difficult word, but it only means that you first select the command about which you want to gain information and then you press **F1**.

If, for instance, you want to get information about column width in this way, proceed as follows:

☞ Press the / key.
☞ Select **Worksheet**.
☞ Select **Column**.
☞ Place the cursor on **Set Width**.
☞ Press **F1**.

Now exactly the same dialog window appears as in the previous example.

Here is a short list of the most important keys in the help screen:

F1   This key will bring you from the help screen back to the main help index screen.

F3   If you press **F3**, you will see a list of all the keys you can use in the help screen.

F8   The **F8** key returns you to the previous help screen.

Esc If you press **Esc** you leave the help screens and return to the worksheet.

What have you learned in this chapter?

In this chapter, you have learned some new features and revised some of the topics you learned in chapter 1. We shall list all the topics here:

- the @AVG function
- saving and retrieving the worksheet
- adjusting the column width and altering the layout
- giving a name to a range
- working with the help function.

Ideas and suggestions

With the functions and possibilities you have learned in this chapter, you can do much more than merely keep track of your school marks. Each time you work something out on paper, think about whether it might be a good idea to create a worksheet.

Also practise giving names to ranges. The subjects column for instance could be given the name 'SUBJECTS'.

3   Extending worksheets

In this chapter you will learn to work with commands which give the worksheet a more professional appearance.

Do you know the answers to the following questions?:

Religious Education

1. Was Samson
   a) a London architect?
   b) a member of Sam's family?
   c) a character from the Bible?

2. Who said "Turn the other cheek"?
   a) Jesus
   b) Madonna
   c) Billy Bunter

3. Is the Devil
   a) an alcoholic drink?
   b) a character from the Bible?
   c) a type of heavy metal music?

Because you are not very good in Religious Education and this is bringing your average down, your parent(s) have promised that you will get a new bike or saxophone if the majority of your marks are 60% or more. If you get 60% or more for a subject, the program will place the word 'Yes' in the adjacent cell.

We shall also illustrate how to place the date in a worksheet each time you load it and how you can align the text.

Finally, you will learn how to sort data so that you can arrange your marks in ascending or descending order.

The @IF() function

Well, school's alright; you can always read magazines in the break. But what we're interested in right now is the bike. We shall use the @IF() function to be able to see at a glance if we have got enough marks. Fill in your school report as shown below, or fill in your own real marks.

	A	B	C	D	E	F	G	H	I	J	K	L	M	N	O	P
	Subject	Written Exams					Oral Exams					Average				
2												(Report %)				
3																
4	English	63	61	58			58	59	64			61				
5	French	59	63	57			58	56	43			57				
6	German	54	63	63			62	56	57			59				
7	Economics	65	57	65			65	45	34			58				
8	History	76	56	65			56	45	65			62				
9	Geography	56	56	56			65	45	55			56				
10	Mathematics	66	56	65			56	54	65			61				
11	Biology	65	56	65			67	55	66			62				
12	Music	77	66	67			67	76	66			70				
13	Technical	44	45	50			55	54	54			49				
14	Health Care	66	65	67			66	56	65			65				
15	Art	66	56	63			63	45	68			61				
16	Handwork	52	48	50			44	54	57			51				
17	Design	59	62	60			60	61	64			61				
18	Religious Ed.	46	52	61			46	39	48			50				
19	Latin	55	61	58			57	61	64			59				
20	Social Std.	67	63	59			59	63	70			63				

I20: 70   READY

16-Jun-94 11:57 AM   NUM

We now want to enter the formula which will display whether or not the magic limit of 60% has been reached. The result will be placed in column N. We shall begin with the first subject, English, in cell N4 and the formula will later be copied downwards to the other cells in this column. The formula is as follows:

```
@IF(L4>=60;"YES!!";"dimwit")
```

The function is constructed as follows: first you specify the condition (sometimes referred to as the *criterion*), in this case the cell contents should be equal to or greater than 60. The second argument is the result which is to be shown if the condition is met. In this case, the word 'YES!!' will be shown if the number in cell L4 is 60 or more.
To let Lotus 1-2-3 know that you want this text to be placed literally in the cell, you have to enclose it in inverted commas.
The last argument in the formula is the text which will be shown if the condition is not met. We have used the word 'dimwit' here, but we might have said 'Work harder!'.

We enter the formula as follows:

☞ Place the cell pointer in cell N4.
☞ Type the formula:

```
@IF(L4>=60;"YES!!";"dimwit")
```

☞ Press **Enter**.

When you have done that, the appropriate text appears in N4. This depends of course on your actual marks.

Copy this formula to the cells below.

☞ Place the cell pointer in N4 if it is not there already.
☞ Press the / key to place the menu bar on the screen.
☞ Select **Copy**.
☞ Press the **Enter** key (the proper cell, N4, is already shown).
☞ Specify the range to which the formula should be copied N5..N21.
☞ Press **Enter**.

The entire column N is now filled with text. Hopefully in your case, the majority will show 'YES!!'. Even if your marks are not all they might be, at least you know how the @IF() function works.

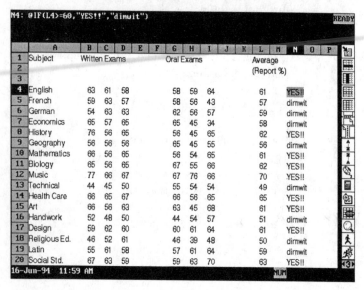

	A	B	C	D	E	F	G	H	I	J	K	L	M	N	O	P	
N4:	@IF(L4>=60,"YES!!","dimwit")														READY		
1	Subject	Written Exams					Oral Exams					Average					
2												(Report %)					
3																	
4	English	63	61	58			58	59	64			61		YES!!			
5	French	59	63	57			58	56	43			57		dimwit			
6	German	54	63	63			62	56	57			59		dimwit			
7	Economics	65	57	65			65	45	34			58		dimwit			
8	History	76	56	65			56	45	65			62		YES!!			
9	Geography	56	56	56			65	45	55			56		dimwit			
10	Mathematics	66	56	65			56	54	65			61		YES!!			
11	Biology	65	56	65			67	55	66			62		YES!!			
12	Music	77	66	67			67	76	66			70		YES!!			
13	Technical	44	45	50			55	54	54			49		dimwit			
14	Health Care	66	65	67			66	56	65			65		YES!!			
15	Art	66	56	63			63	45	68			61		YES!!			
16	Handwork	52	48	50			44	54	57			51		dimwit			
17	Design	59	62	60			60	61	64			61		YES!!			
18	Religious Ed.	46	52	61			46	39	48			50		dimwit			
19	Latin	55	61	58			57	61	64			59		dimwit			
20	Social Std.	67	63	59			59	63	70			63		YES!!			
16-Jun-94 11:59 AM														NUM			

Using the @NOW() function to add the current date to a worksheet

It is very convenient if you can date all your worksheets. If you print out your worksheet, it is clearly stated when you did that. The @NOW() function is ideal for this.

In the REPORT.WK1 worksheet, there is enough room between the title and the name of the subjects to insert the date. We shall do this now.

☞ Place the cell pointer in cell A3.
☞ Type the following:

    @NOW

☞ Press **Enter**.

A large number appears in the cell. Keep cool; Lotus 1-2-3 converts the system time and date in the computer to a number. This number is now shown in the worksheet. If you tell Lotus 1-2-3 that A3 is to be treated as a date cell, this number will be converted to a real date.

☞ Press the / key to open the menu bar.
☞ Select **Range**.
☞ Select **Format**.
☞ Select **Date**.

A whole collection of ways to express the date appears. Select one of them:

☞ Choose for example **1 (DD-MMM-YY)**.
☞ Then press **Enter** since the correct range (A3) is already stated.

Now a real date is placed neatly in A3.

 You can also click on the **Date** icon (icon set 3) to enter the current date in a cell.

(We have removed the date again by placing the cell pointer in the cell and pressing the **Del** key. If you prefer, you can just leave it in your worksheet.)

Signs in front of text

In chapter 2, we mentioned that we would deal with the signs that Lotus 1-2-3 places in front of text which is to be placed in a cell. You can also place these signs there yourself to help Lotus 1-2-3 a little.

You have already noticed that Lotus 1-2-3 automatically places a ' in front of text. If you want to enter a number which is to be treated like a text, such as a telephone number, you will have to place that sign yourself otherwise Lotus 1-2-3 will treat it like a number. This means that the number will be *right-aligned* (placed at the right side of the cell) instead of left-aligned as is the standard setting for text. And if you want to use text, such as a cell address, as a number (the value in the cell), you have to place a + in front of it. We shall make a list of all possible signs along with the corresponding icon if you can select the option using the icon:

' Text is to be left-aligned. In the case of numbers or characters which Lotus 1-2-3 regards as calculation symbols, you indicate that these are to be treated as text.

^ Text is to be centred (placed in the middle of the cell).

" Text is to be right-aligned.

\ (The backslash) If, for instance, you type a backslash and then a dash, the whole cell is filled with dashes. This is an easy way of drawing a stripe in a cell. It also works with letters of course. It is thus a kind of repeat key.

+ Text is to be treated as a number. For example, this sign is used if you begin a formula with a cell address. If you want to calculate using the value in cell A1, type +A1 otherwise the text A1 will be shown.

Moving a column

The screen in our example is getting a bit cluttered. It's difficult to keep our eyes on the right line. In fact what we want to see is the name of the subject and the final Report %.

Fortunately, we can still change the layout. First we shall insert an empty column next to the column containing the subjects, and then we shall move the column containing the final report marks (column L) to the new column so that the final report marks are exactly next to the names of the subjects.

☞ Place the cell pointer anywhere in column B.
☞ Press the / key to open the menu bar.
☞ Select **Worksheet**.
☞ Select **Insert**.
☞ Select **Column**.
☞ Press **Enter**.

You have now inserted an empty column to the left of column B. This new column is now called column B. All the other columns shift up one letter. Lotus 1-2-3 has automatically altered all the column letters in all the formulas. Faster than Linford Christie, not bad eh?

You can now move the contents of column M
(where the report marks now are) to column B.
The **Move** command is used for this.

☞ Place the cell pointer in cell M1.
☞ Press the / key to show the menu bar on the screen.
☞ Select **Move**.
☞ Specify the range you want to move: M1..M22
☞ Press **Enter**.
☞ Type B1 behind 'To where?'.
☞ Press **Enter**.

Now the report marks are next to the subjects.
Unfortunately the text does not fit into the cells B1
and B2 because the standard width has been set to
4. This also applies to the column we inserted. We
shall widen the column:

☞ Place the cell pointer anywhere in cell B.
☞ Press the / to open the menu bar.
☞ Select **Worksheet**.
☞ Select **Column**.
☞ Select **Set-Width**.
☞ Specify the required column width, for example 10.

Now insert a column again to separate the marks.

☞ Place the cell pointer in column C.
☞ Press the / key to open the menu bar.
☞ Select **Worksheet**.
☞ Select **Insert**.
☞ Select **Column**.
☞ The proper column, C, is already filled in so press
  Enter.

Deleting columns

The text at the far right of your screen is almost out of sight. In fact, there is now too much space between the marks and this text. We shall remove the present columns L and M.

☞ Press the / key to open the menu bar.
☞ Select **Worksheet**.
☞ Select **Delete**.
☞ Select **Column**.
☞ Specify the columns to be deleted: L1..M1.

These two columns are deleted, the text shifts to the left and is now displayed in the new column N.

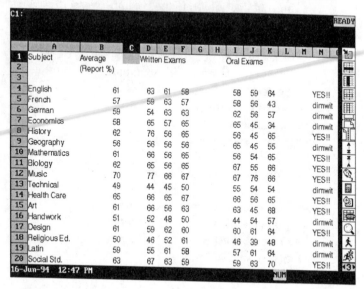

Save the worksheet under the name REPORT.

Sorting

The report is displayed in a rather haphazard way. We shall now put our best foot forward and place our best subjects at the top of the report. In Lotus 1-2-3 you can arrange lists of data in ascending or descending order. We shall place the highest report marks at the top. If there are subjects which have the same mark, we shall sort them in alphabetical order.

The sort key

When you sort data in Lotus 1-2-3, you sort according to a criterion. This could be according to subject for instance; in that case the subjects can be ordered alphabetically in either normal or reverse order.

However, we wish to order the report according to the final report average mark shown in column B. This is the so-called *sort key* in this case.

First you have to sort the area you want to sort. This is done using the **Data** menu.

☞ Press the / key to place the menu bar on the screen.
☞ Select **Data**.

The **Data** submenu is now displayed along the top of the screen.

☞ Select **Sort**.

You do not need to pay much attention to the description in this case (Sort database records) because you can also sort records without defining a database.

A series of menu options is shown along the top of the screen. The first three of these can be specified in the Sort Settings dialog window which is shown in the middle of the screen.

As soon as you press the **Enter** key to select the **Data-Range** option, you can specify the range which is to be sorted. In our case, that is the whole area from A4 to N22; this area contains all our data. Fill this in in the dialog window. When you have done this, this range is displayed in the Data Range section in the dialog window.

☞ Move the cursor to the **Primary-Key** option at the top of the screen.
☞ Press **Enter**.

Now you have to specify the sort key for the report. We wish to sort according to the final average report %, therefore specify column B.

☞ Type **B1**.

Now we have to specify whether the sorting process is to take place in ascending or descending order. We wish to sort in descending order so that the highest marks are shown at the top.

☞ D is also shown. This is what we want.
☞ Press **Enter**.

These specifications are shown in the dialog window. If you accidentally make the wrong settings, press **F2** and then the highlighted letter to alter the setting in question.

There may be one or two subjects in your report which have the same marks. We shall sort these alphabetically. Move the cursor to Secondary-Key at the top of the screen.

☞ Select **Secondary-Key**.
☞ Specify column A as the Secondary sort key. Type **A1**.
☞ Now specify Ascending as the Sort order. Type **A**.

The dialog window now looks like this:

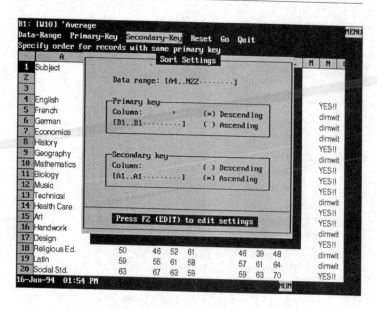

Now you have filled in everything, you can start the
sorting process.

☞ Select **Go** from the top line.

All marks are now sorted in descending order.

Where the marks are similar, the secondary sorting
key has been applied. You may not think so,
because in our example, Maths, Design, Art and
English do not seem to be in alphabetical order. The
reason is that these marks are averages and these
averages have been rounded off by Lotus 1-2-3 to
form whole numbers. But Lotus 1-2-3 is not forget-
ful. The real averages are still stored in memory. We
can show this by looking more closely at the marks.

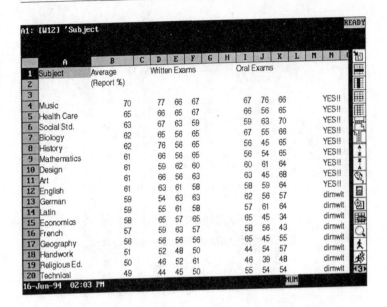

☞ Place the cell pointer in B1.

☞ Press the / key to open the menu bar.

☞ Select **Range**.

☞ Select **Format**.

☞ Select **Fixed**.

☞ Specify **2** decimal places.

☞ Specify the range to format: **B4..B22**.

The precise averages are now shown.

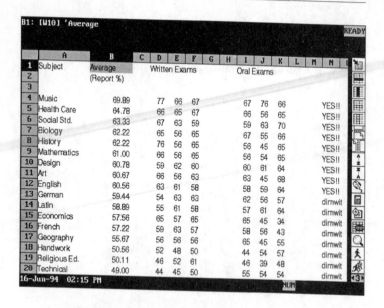

B1: [W10] 'Average   READY

	A	B	C	D	E	F	G	H	I	J	K	L	M	N	
1	Subject	Average		Written Exams				Oral Exams						
2		(Report %)												
3														
4	Music	69.89		77	66	67		67	76	66			YES!!	
5	Health Care	64.78		66	65	67		66	56	65			YES!!	
6	Social Std.	63.33		67	63	59		59	63	70			YES!!	
7	Biology	62.22		65	56	65		67	55	66			YES!!	
8	History	62.22		76	56	65		56	45	65			YES!!	
9	Mathematics	61.00		66	56	65		56	54	65			YES!!	
10	Design	60.78		59	62	60		60	61	64			YES!!	
11	Art	60.67		66	56	63		63	45	68			YES!!	
12	English	60.56		63	61	58		58	59	64			YES!!	
13	German	59.44		54	63	63		62	56	57			dimwit	
14	Latin	58.89		55	61	58		57	61	64			dimwit	
15	Economics	57.56		65	57	65		65	45	34			dimwit	
16	French	57.22		59	63	57		58	56	43			dimwit	
17	Geography	55.67		56	56	56		65	45	55			dimwit	
18	Handwork	50.56		52	48	50		44	54	57			dimwit	
19	Religious Ed.	50.11		46	52	61		46	39	48			dimwit	
20	Technical	49.00		44	45	50		55	54	54			dimwit	

16-Jun-94 02:15 PM   NUM

It is now time to save the worksheet once more. If
you want to save the previous order before the
report was sorted, save this version under a new
name. In that case,

☞ Press / to open the worksheet.
☞ Select **File**.
☞ Select **Save**.
☞ Type the new name, for instance SORTREP.

What have you learned in this chapter?

You have learned a lot in this chapter. We shall make a list:

■ the @IF() function
■ the date function @NOW()
■ the characters which define text alignment
■ moving columns
■ sorting data using the Lotus 1-2-3 database functions.

Ideas and suggestions

You can use the functions you have learned in this chapter when working with other worksheets. For instance, you can use the @IF() function in your CASH worksheet. (If I have more than £7.50 left this month, I will send something to Greenpeace.)

You could also extend your school report with functions which display the absolute highest and lowest marks for all subjects, @MAX() and @MIN().

In the next chapter we shall deal with something completely different. We shall discuss how to create charts and diagrams.

4 Creating charts

One of the attractive features of Lotus 1-2-3 is that you can not only carry out calculations quickly and easily, you can also display them in chart form.

To give an example of this, we shall create a simple worksheet representing bicycling speeds. Then we shall create the chart with an X and Y axis, titles and explanation. We use bicycling speeds, but you could use swimming times or scores in your computer games etc. Once you have worked through this example, it will be quite easy to create a chart representing data in another worksheet.

Create the worksheet

We shall first create the worksheet containing the data about the number of miles we cycle and the time it takes. We shall then get Lotus 1-2-3 to work out the average speed which we shall use to create the chart.

If you have a racing bike, you will want to know if you have a chance of being invited to take part in the Tour de France.

We shall start with the following figures:

Bicycling speed

distance (miles)	time (min.)
7	30
8	38
7	33
10	52
7	32
12	64

We shall enter these data in a new worksheet.
Open a new worksheet as explained at the beginning of chapter 2.

Then enter the data as shown above, or enter your
own personal data. Remember when entering the
brackets to type an apostrophe first so that Lotus
1-2-3 recognises these as text, otherwise it will
expect a formula. The worksheet will look something like this:

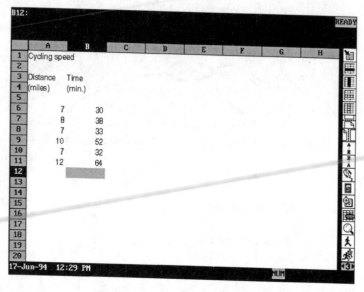

We shall now create a column next to these
columns, in which the number of miles per hour is
recorded. To do this, we shall use a formula to
calculate the speed based on the figures in columns
A and B.

☞ Place the cell pointer in cell C6.

☞ Type the following formula:

    (A6/B6)*60

☞ Press **Enter**.

The distance cycled is divided by the time taken to calculate the distance travelled in one minute; this is then multiplied by 60 to calculate the distance that would be travelled in one hour. In our example that is 14 miles per hour.

Now copy this formula to the cells below:

☞ Place the cell pointer in cell C6.
☞ Press the / key to open the menu bar.
☞ Select **Copy**.
☞ Press **Enter** since the correct cell is already filled in.
☞ Specify the range C7..C11 behind the question 'To where?'.
☞ Press **Enter**.

The average speed is now shown for each distance. There are many figures behind the decimal point. We shall alter this.

☞ Place the cell pointer in C6.
☞ Press the / key to open the menu bar.
☞ Select **Range**.
☞ Select **Format**.
☞ Select **Fixed**.
☞ Specify the required number of decimal places: **1**.
☞ Press **Enter**.
☞ Specify the range C6..C11.
☞ Press **Enter**.

The numbers in column C now all have one decimal place. This is sufficient for our worksheet which now looks like this:

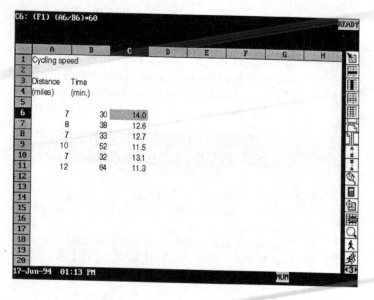

We shall now make a chart of this simple worksheet. Just to be safe we shall save the worksheet first.

☞ Press the / key to open the menu bar.
☞ Select **File**.
☞ Select **Save**.
☞ Type a name for the file, for instance:

CYCLE

☞ Press **Enter**.

You have now returned to the worksheet and the
data have been saved. If anything does go wrong,
you can always start at this point again.

Creating the chart

To create the chart, you use the **Graph** menu. As
soon as you activate this menu, the Graph Settings
dialog window appears.

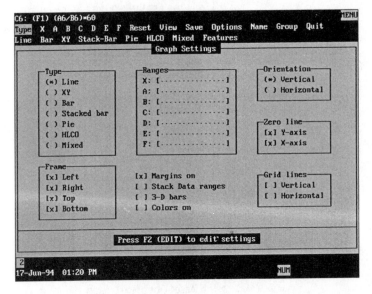

All the options in the **Graph** menu are displayed
along the top of the screen. We shall examine them
one by one, so that you can get to know what each
option does. All the settings that you specify when
working with a given option are shown in the
Graph Settings dialog window itself.

option	significance
Type	The **Type** option determines what type of chart you want to create. You can choose Line diagram, Bar chart, XY diagram, Stack bar chart, Pie chart, High-Low-Close-Open diagram (used for stock markets) or Mixed diagram. The most suitable option depends on the sort of data you want to display. Using the **Features** option at the end of the line, you can define options to improve the appearance of the diagram. For instance, **3D-Effect** will give your chart a three-dimensional appearance.
X	At **X**, you specify the range which is to be used as the values for the X axis in your chart. Lotus 1-2-3 refers to this as the 'X range'.
A..F	The other ranges, **A** to **F**, are used to specify the values which are to be used as the values for the Y axis. Thus, there can be six different ranges in total.
Reset	If you make a mistake, you can select the **Reset** option to specify different settings for the type of chart, the X range, the A to F ranges etc.
View	The chart is shown on the screen when you select **View**.

Save   If you select **Save**, the chart is saved in a
                        file. You can print this file later so that
                        you can get a graph on paper.

Options   **Options** opens a large submenu with all
                        kinds of elements which you can use for
                        the chart. You can add a legend to the
                        chart or titles to explain the data. It is
                        also possible to set a grid or adjust the
                        scale of the chart.

Name   Use the **Name** option to give the chart
                        a name. This is different to saving it. It is
                        more like giving a name to a range as
                        we did in chapter 2. You can create
                        several charts within one worksheet and
                        by giving each its own name, you can
                        distinguish them from one another. We
                        shall do this shortly.

Group   If you wish to set several data ranges in
                        one go, you should define them as
                        being one group. The **group** option is
                        used for this.

Quit   If you have completed the settings for
                        your chart and want to return to the
                        worksheet, choose **Quit**.

As you see, there are quite a few possibilities for
creating the desired type of chart.

Before actually beginning, it is advisable to think
about which type of chart is most suitable for dis-
playing the data.

Average speed = 0

Creating a bar chart

We shall first create a chart in which the distance is
displayed in relation to the time. The bar chart is
suitable for doing this.

☞ In the **Graph** menu, select **Type**.
☞ Select **Bar**.
☞ Select **X**.
☞ Specify A6..A11 as the range.
☞ Select **A**.
☞ Specify the range as B6..B11.

Now examine the result.

☞ Select **View**.

The result is a clear diagram with the data from column A as the X axis (horizontal). The Y axis (vertical) has been neatly divided to show the data figures. This division is called *scaling*.

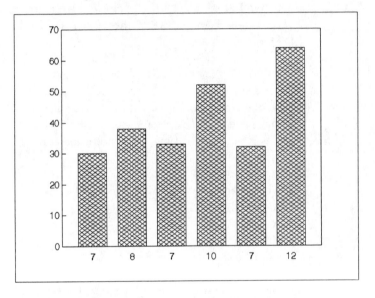

Unfortunately, the chart is not very informative yet. We shall make alterations so that it provides more information.

By pressing any key, you return to the **Graph** sub-menu and the Graph Settings dialog window.

If you want to change a setting, you can select the option which deals with that setting and make the specifications all over again. But you can also change the settings in the Graph Settings window. To do

this, press **F2**, the EDIT key. This activates the dialog
window. You will see that some letters are shown in
bold or in another colour. If you type this letter, you
will activate the corresponding section in the dialog
window. For instance, if you have specified a range
for the X axis and you wish to change this, press **F2**
and then **R** (for Ranges). The Range letters are now
accentuated. Press X to select the X range and fill in
the required range.

We shall presume that the chart is as it should be.
But as mentioned, we wish to add explanations to
make the graph more informative. It would be
helpful if we could see what the X and the Y axis
represent and a title above the chart would also
provide clarity.

The commands we need are to be found in the
Options submenu.

☞ Select **Options**.
☞ Select **Titles**.

Another dialog window is displayed on the screen.
This will show the text that you specify for the chart.
This dialog window is the Graph Legends & Titles
window.

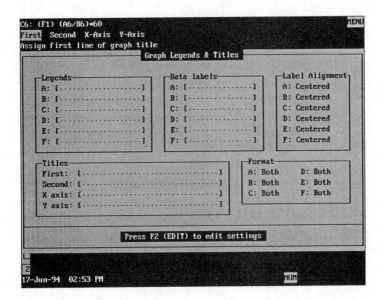

In the **Titles** section there are options for explanations and titles. We shall give a main title to the chart.

☞ Select **First** from the menu bar.
☞ Type behind 'Enter first line of graph title:' the text you want to place there, such as:

```
Cycling speed
```

☞ Press **Enter**.

We shall not enter anything behind **Second**, but if you do want to place a secondary title (like 'summer '94'), that is done here. We now only want to add explanations for the X and Y axes.

☞ Select **Titles**.
☞ Select **X-Axis**.
☞ Type behind 'Enter x-axis title' the text:

```
number of miles
```

☞ Press **Enter**.
☞ Select **Titles**.
☞ Select **Y-Axis**.
☞ Type behind 'Enter y-axis title' the text:

```
number of minutes
```

By pressing **Quit** you return to the **Graph** main
menu. Select **View** to have a look at the chart.

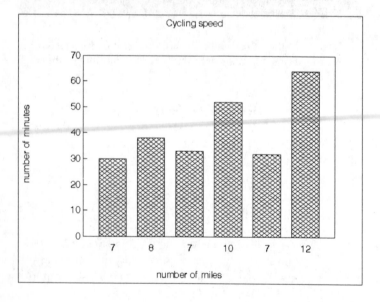

This is a bit better. But we still cannot get very much information from the chart. We need column C which displays the average speed. The entire chart should be shown in mixed form, with the previous chart as the basis; column C will be displayed as a line running through this chart.

Accordingly, we shall create a mixed chart. We shall do this in the next section. First press any key to return to the **Graph** options.

Giving the chart a name

We shall now give the chart a name so that we can always fall back on this stored version if something goes wrong in the following exercise.

When you give a chart a name , the current settings
of the chart are saved.

☞ Select **Name**.

As you see, a submenu appears providing five
options. We shall give a small explanation of these
options:

Use — If you select **Use**, a list appears showing the
names which you have given to previous
charts. Select the name of the chart with
which you wish to work.

Create — If you want to give the current chart a name,
select **Create**. Don't forget that if you change
a setting and you wish to save it, you have to
select this option again and give the same
name to the chart.

Delete — The **Delete** option removes the chart you
specify. The graph settings are thus also lost.

Reset — The **Reset** option sounds less dangerous than
it actually is. It really means that the original
settings in the program are restored and all
charts to which you have given a name will
be deleted. Therefore be very careful.
Fortunately Lotus 1-2-3 warns you a couple of
times before the deletion takes place.
Nevertheless, you have to pay attention if
you don't want to lose all your hard work.

Table — If you have created lots of charts and have
given them all names, select **Table**. In that
case, you can place a list in a worksheet,
showing all the names of these charts.

Now you know what all these options do, you can
choose the right one:

☞ Select **Create**.
☞ Type a name, for instance:

BICYCLE

☞ Press **Enter**.

You have now saved the settings of this chart, and
you can retrieve these settings whenever you like
by selecting the **Use** option from the **Name** submenu. Try it out to see if the chart really does appear on the screen.

Creating a mixed chart

Before creating a mixed chart, we shall return to the
worksheet containing our data. We shall begin the
chart process all over again. Press **Esc** a number of
times to return to the worksheet.

☞ Press the / key to open the menu bar.
☞ Select **Graph**.
☞ Select **Reset**.
☞ Select **Graph**.

Now you have deleted all other settings and we can
begin all over again. We are now sure that any
previous settings will not influence the chart we are
now going to make.

☞ Select **Type**.
☞ Select **Mixed** by moving to it using the cursor and pressing **Enter**.
☞ Select **X** and type the required range, A6..A11.
☞ Select **A** and specify B6..B11.
☞ Select **D** and specify C6..C11.

Yes, you have read it correctly, it was **D**. In a mixed chart the first three ranges (A, B and C) are used for bars and the other three (D, E and F) are used for lines.

Look at the interim result.

☞ Select **View**.

The average speed is shown as a line across the columns. The line is reasonably straight which indicates your fitness is pretty constant.

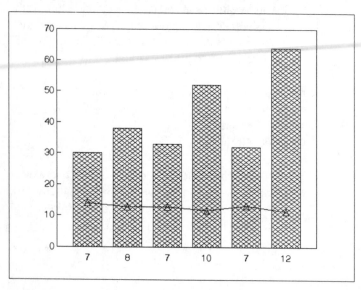

We shall also make this chart more attractive. This will help make the information clearer. But we shall take care not to make the chart too cluttered because that may give a chaotic impression. The best charts are those from which you can gain the necessary information at a glance.

Therefore, do not just add things at random, make a plan first.

Legends

Because we now have two data ranges in the chart, we should add explanations (so-called *legends*) which indicate which signs are being used for which data.

☞ First press any key to return to the input screen.
☞ Select **Options**.
☞ Select **Legend**.
☞ Select **A**.
☞ Behind 'Enter legend for first data range:' type the text

```
miles
```

☞ Press **Enter**.
☞ Select **Legend** again.
☞ Select **D**.
☞ Behind 'Enter legend for fourth data range:' type the text

```
average speed
```

☞ Press **Enter**.

We shall now look at the result.

☞ Select **Quit**.
☞ Select **View**.

The following chart is shown:

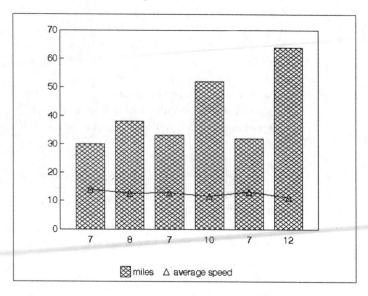

Return to the input screen by pressing any key.

Titles

Just as with the previous chart, we shall also give a title to this one.

☞ Select **Options**.

Het Spectrum

P.O. Box 2996

London N5 2TA

Be an expert! **BOOKS REPLY CARD**

Please send me further information on other titles in the *Be an expert!* series.

Name: ....

Address: ....

....

Postcode: ....

This internationally successful series of computer books for young people provides comprehensive, step-by-step courses that are suitable for the home or school at an affordable price.

☞ Select **Titles**.
☞ Select **First**.
☞ Type a title for the chart, for instance:

```
Average bicycling speed
```

☞ Press **Enter**.

Now give the X axis an explanation.

☞ Select **Titles**.
☞ Select **X-Axis**.
☞ Type an explanation of the X axis, for instance:

```
number of miles
```

☞ Press **Enter**.

Give the Y axis an explanation as well.

☞ Select **Titles**.
☞ Select **Y-Axis**.
☞ Type an explanation of the Y axis, for instance:

```
number of minutes
```

☞ Press **Enter**.

We shall now have a quick look at the result to see
if everything has gone correctly.

☞ Select **Quit**.
☞ Select **View**.

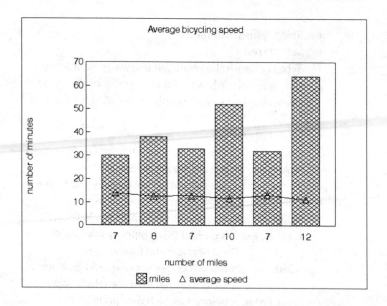

You may have noticed that our chart does not completely explain the facts. Have a good look. The Y axis displays the **number of minutes** and also the **number of miles per hour**. In fact, it would be convenient if we were to have two Y axes to display this, but unfortunately this is not possible. That being the case, we should really change the axis title to 'number of minutes/miles per hour'. As you will realize, mixed diagrams can be quite complicated.

However, the chart is alright as it is; we don't want to make it more cluttered.

We shall now deal with the **Options** submenu so that you can become familiar with the possibilities if you want to create another chart yourself.

The Options submenu

This command has quite an extensive submenu. You have already worked with some of the options there, but just to be complete, we shall list them all below:

Legend	You already know this option. This enables you to add a legend to your chart.
Format	The **Format** option enables you to draw lines or place symbols in your chart.
Titles	You also already know the **Titles** option. It enables you to specify titles for the entire graph and for the axes.
Grid	It is sometimes useful to add gridlines to a chart. You can then see which values belong to which data points.
Scale	If you are not happy about the way Lotus 1-2-3 has arranged the chart on the screen, choose the **Scale** option. You can then make the intervals greater or smaller to represent the data as you would like.
Color	If you have a colour screen, you can select the **Color** option to display charts in colour on the screen. If you have a colour printer, the chart can be then printed in colour.
B&W	Choosing this option means that you will display the chart in black-and-white. It will also be printed in black-and-white.
Data-Labels	If you want to show the actual values next to the data points in a chart, select **Data-Labels**.
Quit	**Quit** will return you to the **Graph** menu.

Giving the chart a name and saving it

It is now time to give the chart a name and to save it on disk.

Giving the chart a name

If you give the chart a name, you can retrieve the chart later and alter it when you are working in the same worksheet. We mentioned this when creating the previous chart. If you also give this chart a name, you will have one worksheet with two charts.

☞ Select **Name**.
☞ Select **Create**.
☞ Type a name for the chart, for instance:

BICYCLE1

☞ Press **Enter**.

Saving the chart as a file

Of course, you will want to print the chart later to let the local cycling club see that you are a promising candidate for the Tour de France. To do this, you first have to save the chart as a file.

Proceed as follows:

☞ In the **Graph** menu, select **Save**.
☞ Type a name for the file, for instance:

```
BICYCLE1
```

☞ Press **Enter**.

It is convenient to give the file to be printed the same name as the chart so there will be no confusion.

Lotus 1-2-3 automatically adds the extension PIC behind the file name. Lotus 1-2-3 then recognizes the file as a graphic file.

We shall deal with printing a graphic file in chapter 6.

Saving the worksheet

Finally save the entire worksheet, otherwise you will lose everything except the graphic file. This is of course not our intention.

☞ Select **Quit**.
☞ Press the/ key to open the menu bar.
☞ Select **File**.
☞ Select **Save**.
☞ Press **Enter** (the name of the file is already shown).
☞ Select **Replace**.

What have you learned in this chapter?

We shall make a list of what we have learned:

- creating normal charts
- creating mixed charts
- adding features to a chart, such as titles and legends
- giving a chart a name
- saving a chart.

Ideas and suggestions

The basic skills you have learned in this chapter enable you to make other charts. Use the BICYCLE chart to try out the other types of charts available. Select **Type** in the **Graph** menu. Then select one after the other **Line, Bar** etc. Use **View** each time to examine the result.

You could also use the data from the average speed to work out how long it would approximately take you to cycle a different distance, for example 15 miles or 20 miles.

5 WYSIWYG: making worksheets and charts more attractive

The worksheet we used to display the school report in chapter 2 was quite efficient. But we cannot really say that it was very attractive in appearance. We did make some alterations to improve it but that did not amount to much. The chart we created in the previous chapter was also OK, but it could be much better.

In this chapter, we shall illustrate how you can use the *WYSIWYG* module to improve the appearance of your worksheets and charts. This can be done in many ways, for instance by placing the text in bold letters or by putting frames around cell data or by changing the size and type of letters being used.

To begin with, we shall display the school report on the screen again.

☞ Press the / key to open the menu bar.
☞ Select **File**.
☞ Select **Retrieve**.
☞ Move the cursor to **REPORT.WK1**.
☞ Press **Enter**.

The REPORT worksheet is now displayed on the screen.

The WYSIWYG module (What You See Is What You Get)

Up until now you have pressed the / key to open the menu bar. But there is also another key you can use to produce a completely different menu:

☞ Press the : key (the colon).

(Hold down the **Shift** key and press the key showing the colon and semi-colon.)

A menu bar is opened at the top of the screen but it has different menus than those you are used to.

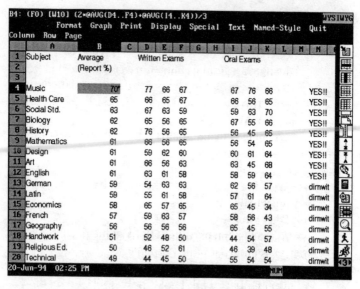

Do you know what you have done? You have opened the Lotus 1-2-3 WYSIWYG module. This module (which means a particular way of working)

is meant for improving and refining the appearance of your charts and worksheets. It is in fact a separate module, but it is placed on the harddisk during the installation so that you can use it straightaway.

The term WYSIWYG means that what comes out of your printer when you print worksheets or charts closely resembles that which is shown on the screen.

Once you have opened this menu in the normal way (by pressing the : key), it will subsequently always open as soon as you move the mouse pointer to the menu area. This also applies to the normal menu. Lotus 1-2-3 opens the menu you last used.

We shall give a brief description of all menus in the WYSIWYG module so that you can get an impression of this module. Then we shall apply a few of these options to improve the appearance of our worksheet.

When we have done that, we shall also get to grips with the chart from the previous chapter.

But first the menus:

menu	significance
Worksheet	Using the options from the **Worksheet** menu, you can set the column width and row height, and make page breaks.
Format	The **Format** menu provides many options. You can choose a different letter type (called *font* in Lotus 1-2-3), or

have the text in boldface, italics or underlined. You can alter the colours, add lines, gives shading to certain ranges etc.

Graph   The **Graph** menu provides options for creating and modifying charts. You can also place a chart next to a worksheet on the screen, you can alter or move the chart and much more. We shall devote a whole section to improving the appearance of charts.

Print   The **Print** menu is used to make settings for actually printing the worksheet or chart. We shall deal with this menu and relevant matters in the next chapter.

Display   Using the **Display** menu options, you can specify the way in which the worksheet is shown on the screen. For example, if you think that the cells are rather small, choose the **Zoom** option; this enables you to enlarge the cell display. The **Mode** option enables you to switch back and forward between the graphic display mode and the text mode, or between colour and black-and-white display.

Special   As the name indicates, **Special** provides special options. They enable you to copy or move the WYSIWYG format you have used to other ranges or save them in a file.

Text   The options from the **Text** menu enable you to carry out all kinds of text procedures such as aligning text or converting numbers to text.

Named-Style   Perhaps you are already familiar with WordPerfect and you know the term *style*. If you have given a cell (or range of cells) a number of features and you want to give the same features to another cell (or range of cells), give a name to the formatting features you have given to the cell(s). This is then a style. This is done by means of the **Define** option. If you want to use the style for other cells, select one of the options **1** to **8**.

Quit   When you choose **Quit**, you return to the READY mode, the normal worksheet screen in Lotus 1-2-3.

Improving the worksheet appearance

After all this dry theory, it's time we got down to using some of these interesting options in our worksheet. You have seen that there is enough choice.

Data in boldface

The titles in the report, thus the data in the first row, are to be given more emphasis. This can be done by using bold, italics or underlining for instance.

We shall change the titles to boldface (italics and underlining are also applied in a similar way).

☞ Place the cell pointer in cell A1.
☞ Press the : key to display the WYSIWYG menu on the screen.
☞ Select **Format**.
☞ Select **Bold**.
☞ Select **Set**.
☞ Specify the range A1..N2.
☞ Press **Enter**.

All titles have now been converted to boldface. When the cell pointer is situated in any of these cells, '{Bold}' is shown at the top left-hand corner of the screen.

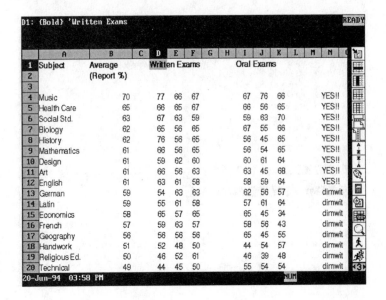

D1: {Bold} 'Written Exams

	A	B	C	D	E	F	G	H	I	J	K	L	M	N
1	Subject	Average		Written Exams					Oral Exams					
2		(Report %)												
3														
4	Music	70		77	66	67			67	76	66			YES!!
5	Health Care	65		66	65	67			66	56	65			YES!!
6	Social Std.	63		67	63	59			59	63	70			YES!!
7	Biology	62		65	56	65			67	55	66			YES!!
8	History	62		76	56	65			56	45	65			YES!!
9	Mathematics	61		66	56	65			56	54	65			YES!!
10	Design	61		59	62	60			60	61	64			YES!!
11	Art	61		66	56	63			63	45	68			YES!!
12	English	61		63	61	58			58	59	64			YES!!
13	German	59		54	63	63			62	56	57			dimwit
14	Latin	59		55	61	58			57	61	64			dimwit
15	Economics	58		65	57	65			65	45	34			dimwit
16	French	57		59	63	57			58	56	43			dimwit
17	Geography	56		56	56	56			65	45	55			dimwit
18	Handwork	51		52	48	50			44	54	57			dimwit
19	Religious Ed.	50		46	52	61			46	39	48			dimwit
20	Technical	49		44	45	50			55	54	54			dimwit

READY

20-Jun-94 03:58 PM   NUM

Font and font size

The final report marks are shown alongside the
exam results. It would be better if the final report
marks also received more emphasis. We shall make
these marks a little larger.

☞ Place the cell pointer in B4.
☞ Press the : key to open the WYSIWYG menu.
☞ Select **Format**.
☞ Select **Font**.

A dialog window appears with the name 'Wysiwyg
Font Selection'. This dialog window enables you to
choose a different font.

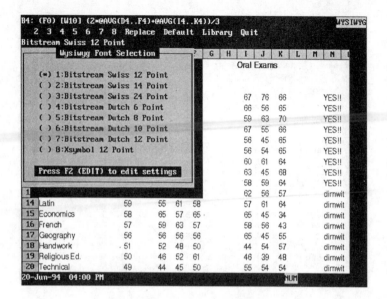

The eight standard fonts which are allocated to the first eight options can be directly selected by pressing the corresponding number. The standard (default) setting is the Bitstream Swiss 12 point font. Because you want to emphasize the final marks, we shall increase the size of the numbers to 24 points, for example.

☞ Select **3**.
☞ Specify the range to which the new point size is to apply, B4..B22.

You will now return to the normal worksheet which now shows numbers like road signs.

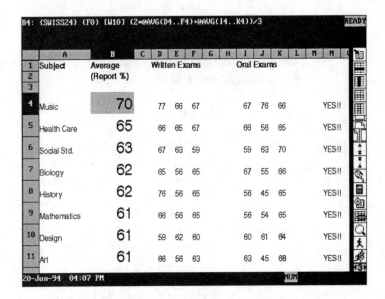

The height of the cells has also been automatically adjusted. The text in the top left-hand corner {SWISS24} indicates that the default settings have been changed.

Lines and frames

It would make our report more legible if there were boxes for each mark.

For this kind of job, Lotus 1-2-3 has the **Lines** option which is to be found in the **Format** menu of the WYSIWYG mode.

☞ Press the : key to open the WYSIWYG menu.
☞ Select **Format**.
☞ Select **Lines**.

A submenu appears with a great number of options. Since you will probably use these options somewhere in other worksheets, we shall give a brief explanation of their functions:

option	significance
Outline	The **Outline** option enables you to place a single line around the entire specified range. A frame is thus placed around the data.
Left, Right, Top, Bottom	These options enable you to place a line at the left- or right-hand side, top or bottom of each cell in the selected range.
All	If you want to place a frame around all the cells in a range, select this option.
Double	Select this option if you want to draw a double line. You can also specify if it is to be drawn at the top, bottom, left- or right-hand side of a cell, or all around.
Wide	An extra thick line is drawn if you specify this option.
Clear	If, in retrospect, you find the lines too thick or if you are not satisfied with the result, use the **Clear** option to remove the lines.
Shadow	The **Shadow** option will also produce an attractive effect. This places a shadowline alongside a cell or range of cells.

Having read through this list, you will probably have concluded that the option we want is **All**.

☞ Select **All**.

☞ Now specify the range in which the lines are to be drawn, D4..K20

☞ Press **Enter**.

The entire range is now divided into boxes.

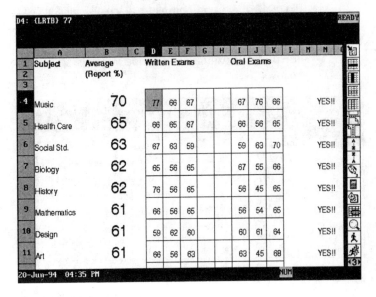

If you have more marks in your report, you can insert rows as you please and create extra boxes in the same way.

You are now probably getting an idea of all the interesting possibilities in this menu. You could place, for instance, a double line under the titles:

☞ Place the cell pointer in cell A2.
☞ Press the : key to open the WYSIWYG menu.
☞ Select **Format**.
☞ Select **Lines**.
☞ Select **Double**.

☞ Select **Bottom**.

☞ Specify the range where you want to have the double line, thus A2..N2.

☞ Press **Enter**.

To make the report complete, place a single line under the other cells in the report. We shall not explain this in detail because this is done just as in the previous exercise. The report will then appear as follows:

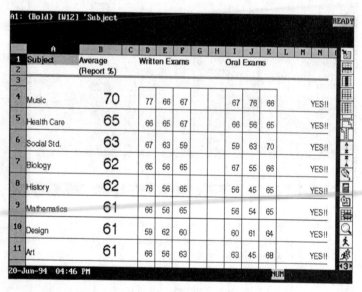

The background

Finally, we shall conclude this section about the formatting possibilities with information about how you can alter the background colour of a cell.

We shall give the title of the report a red background:

☞ Place the cell pointer in cell A1.
☞ Press the : key to open the WYSIWYG menu.
☞ Select **Format**.
☞ Select **Color**.
☞ Select **Background**.
☞ Select **Red**.
☞ Specify the range which is to be given a red background, thus A1..N2.
☞ Press **Enter**.

The screen will look something like this (but in colour):

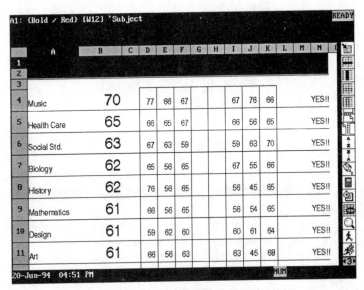

During this selection, you will have noticed the many possibilities you have for setting the colours.

You can allocate colours to both the text in a cell
and to the cell background, and having done that,
you can choose from seven different colours. If you
are working with a black-and-white screen, Lotus
1-2-3 converts these colours into different patterns.

After all these adjustments, save the worksheet
once more. We shall not make any further changes.

Making a chart more attractive

Using the WYSIWYG module, you can improve the
appearance of not only a worksheet but also of a
chart. We shall see what we can do with the BICY-
CLE1 chart.

Load the CYCLE.WK1 file on the screen. This is the
worksheet in which you created the BICYCLE1
chart.

To improve the appearance of the chart we shall
make use of the options provided by the **Graph**
menu in the WYSIWYG module.

☞ Press the : key to open the WYSIWYG menu.
☞ Select **Graph**.

We shall now give a brief explanation of the options
in this menu. We shall not use them all in the exercise we are about to carry out, but at least you will
become acquainted with their function. When practising further with your own worksheets, you will
know which option to choose.

option	significance
Add	The **Add** option places a chart in the worksheet. The you have both the chart and the data on the screen. You can specify where you want to have the chart on the screen. The size is adjusted automatically.
Remove	If you have added a chart to a worksheet and you want to remove it again, select **Remove**. The chart is not really lost, but it is no longer shown in the worksheet.
Goto	Use the **Goto** option to move quickly to a chart in a worksheet. This is done by specifying the cell address of the chart.
Settings	You can determine many features of the chart using the **Settings** option. You can replace the chart, adjust the size, switch the recalculation function on or off, make the graph opaque or transparent etc.
Move	If you have placed a graph in a worksheet but are not satisfied with its position, use the **Move** option to position it elsewhere.
Zoom	If you have placed a chart in a worksheet alongside the data, you probably will not have much space for the chart. In that case it may be difficult to read the data in the chart. If you want to have a close look at these data, use the **Zoom** option to enlarge the chart to fill the screen.
Compute	The **Compute** option is used to redraw the chart to accommodate new data that you have entered in the worksheet.
View	If you wish to see a different chart which you have saved as a file, select the **View** option. The chart you select will be shown full screen.

Edit   The **Edit** option is very extensive, providing
              many options for altering a chart. You can
              add elements to a chart, such as text, a line
              or an arrow and then make modifications to
              these elements. You can also use various
              colours and shapes for diverse components
              in a chart. The **Options** option in this menu
              enables you for instance to add gridlines to
              a chart or to adjust the size of the cell point-
              er in the chart window. You can also adjust
              the size of the text in the chart.

Quit   You are already familiar with this option. It
              brings you back to the Lotus 1-2-3 input
              screen.

So, as you see, there are many possibilities for
improving the appearance of a chart.

We shall first place the chart which belongs to the
CYCLE.WK1 worksheet on the screen alongside the
data.

☞ Select **Add** from the **Graph** menu.
☞ Select the **Named** option from the submenu.

The names of the charts you made are now shown,
BICYCLE and BICYCLE1.

☞ Select BICYCLE1.

Now you have to specify the range where the chart
is to be placed. You have a lot of space at the right-
hand side so that the chart has enough room if
placed there. The larger the range, the more clearly
the chart will be displayed.

☞ Specify the range D1..H13.

☞ Press **Enter**.

The chart is now shown neatly next to the data in the worksheet; everything is shown simultaneously on the screen.

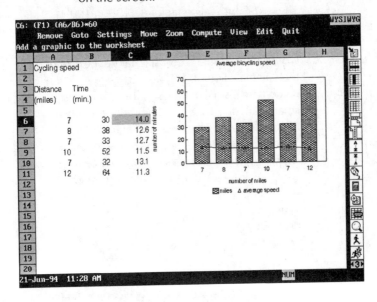

Looks not bad, eh?

Enlarging the text

Because the chart is only shown on half a screen, the texts are not easily readable. We shall make them a little larger.

☞ Press the : key to place the WYSIWYG menu on the screen.

☞ Select **Graph**.
☞ Select **Edit**.
☞ Specify the cell address of the chart, D1.
☞ Now select **Options**.
☞ Select **Font-Magnification**.

The text 'Font scaling factor (0..1000): 100' is shown at the top of the screen. This means that the text is being displayed in 100% format, in other words, normal size. You can change the size here by typing a value other than 100.
If you type a smaller number, the text becomes smaller. If you type a greater number, the text becomes larger. This does not influence the size of the chart. However, if you make the letters too large, they will be pressed on top of one another which makes it even more difficult to read.

☞ Type 150.
☞ Press **Enter**.
☞ Select **Quit**.

The worksheet appears again along with the chart and adjusted text which is now clearly legible. You will notice that the values shown on the X and Y axes have also been enlarged. Lotus 1-2-3 enlarges thus all the texts in a chart.

Adding elements

It might be a good idea to emphasize the data point showing the highest average cycling speed. We shall do this by placing an arrow there. In Lotus 1-2-3 this is called *adding an object*.

☞ Press the : key to open the WYSIWYG menu.
☞ Select **Graph**.
☞ Select **Edit**.
☞ Specify the chart address, D1.
☞ Select **Add**.
☞ Select **Arrow**.

The screen undergoes a quick change. Values are
shown at the top behind X and Y, and the cell pointer has changed into a cross. If you move the mouse
or the cursor keys, you will see that the values
behind X and Y also change. These values indicate
the current co-ordinates of the cell pointer.
The easiest way of drawing an arrow is to use the
mouse but you can also do it using the cursor keys
and Enter or by typing the required co-ordinates
(which produces a very precise arrow but is more
difficult to estimate).

☞ Place the cursor above the first bar, somewhere
between the 40 and the 50.
☞ Press **Enter** or press the left mouse button and hold
it down.
☞ Now draw a line (diagonally) downwards by pressing the cursor keys or by moving the mouse to the
required position at the data point.
☞ Press **Enter** or click with the mouse.

If you have done everything as we have outlined
above, an arrow will now point to the data point
showing the highest average speed.

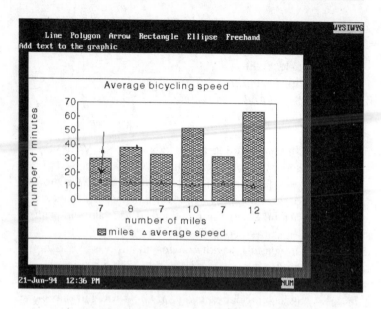

☞ Press **Esc** until you return to the worksheet.

The arrow is clearly shown on the normal screen.

Adding text

Because you created the chart, you know what this arrow means. But others probably do not. It would be useful if you could place a small explanation next to the arrow for the benefit of others.

☞ Press the : key to open the WYSIWYG menu.
☞ Select **Graph**.
☞ Select **Edit**.
☞ Specify the cell address of the chart, D1.
☞ Select **Add**.
☞ Select **Text**.

You can now type text behind the word 'Text:' at
the top of the screen. This text will shortly be added
to the chart.

☞ Type TOP.
☞ Press **Enter**.

On the screen a cursor appears in the form of the
text you have just typed. You can move this text
and place at the required position by pressing the
cursor keys or moving the mouse.

☞ Place the text next to the arrow.
☞ Press **Enter** or click with the mouse.

You have now positioned the text (although you
can still move it by clicking on it with the mouse
and dragging it to another position).

Adding frames

We shall now place a frame around the text you
have just added. Because all the frames we have
used up until now have been rectangular, we shall
use an oval one here just to be different.

We assume that the previous menu is still on the
screen.

☞ Select **Add**.
☞ Select **Ellipse**.

The cursor again changes into a cross.

☞ Draw a frame around the word TOP by pressing the left mouse button, holding it down and moving the mouse so that the word is enclosed. You can also do this by moving the cursor keys until the cross is at the first corner and then pressing **Enter**. Now press the cursor keys so that the word is enclosed.

☞ Press **Enter**.

The rectangle changes into an oval. The final result will appear as follows:

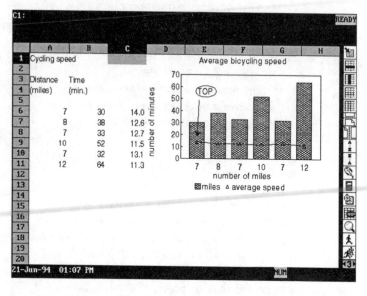

We have not been able to deal with all the available possibilities, but you have probably been able to get an idea of what can be done. Just as we did with the worksheet, you could also use colours here too in order to give the chart special effects. But the chart should not become more cluttered than it already is; this will only spoil the effect. We shall therefore save it as it is.

☞ Press the / key to open the menu bar.
☞ Select **File**.
☞ Select **Save**.
☞ Press **Enter** to accept the current name
☞ Select **Replace**.

What have you learned in this chapter?

This was quite a heavy chapter. We shall make a list of the topics we have discussed:

- WYSIWYG
- improving the worksheet appearance
  - showing data in boldface
  - changing the font and font size
  - adding lines and frames
  - changing the background colour
- making the chart more attractive
  - adjusting the text
  - adding various objects.

Now that you have made the worksheet and chart so attractive, it would be nice to have it all on paper. The following chapter deals with printing.

Ideas and suggestions

Remember the worksheet you made in the first chapter? Perhaps you could improve the appearance of the worksheet and see if you can create a chart (a pie chart for example) to show the percentages of your expenditure.

6   Printing

Up until now you have had output on the screen
only. But if you want to let someone else see your
excellent work, it's often much easier to put a piece
of paper in your bag or pocket than your computer.

In this chapter, we shall deal with the possibilities
available when printing. You can make a large number of settings. There is also a difference between
printing a normal worksheet, a worksheet you have
designed using the WYSIWYG module and printing
a chart.

Printing worksheets and charts

In the previous chapters, you have created various
worksheets and charts. We shall make use of these
to illustrate how to go about printing.

Printing the standard worksheet

We shall first deal with how to print a normal worksheet. We shall use the CASH.WK1 worksheet for
this. We have to retrieve it first.

☞ Press the / key to open the menu bar.
☞ Select **File**.
☞ Select **Retrieve**.
☞ Select CASH.WK1.

The worksheet is now shown on the screen.

Before printing, we shall first check to see if the general print settings in Lotus 1-2-3 are correct.

☞ Press the / key to open the menu bar.

☞ Select **Worksheet**.

☞ Select **Global**.

☞ Select **Default**.

☞ Select **Printer**.

The screen now shows the large dialog window, Default Printer Settings, which contains the current printer settings.

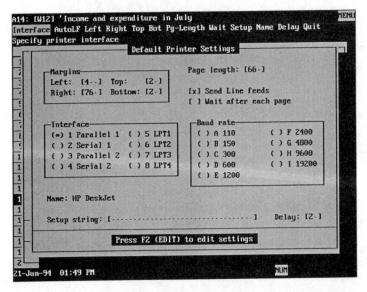

The most important setting at this moment is what is shown behind 'Name:'. If the text 'No printer installed' is shown, then it will not be possible to print. Normally a name will be displayed here, because during the installation of Lotus 1-2-3 you can specify which printer you are going to work with.

The other information in this dialog window refers to the margins, the page length and the interface (the port, in other words, the output channel at the back of the computer, which is connected to the printer).

Leave this window by selecting **Quit** twice. Now you know that a printer is installed and that you can begin printing.

Printing a normal worksheet is done using the **Print** menu. Switch the printer on and make sure that there is enough paper.

☞ Press the / key to open the menu bar.
☞ Select **Print**.
☞ Select **Printer**.

A dialog window now appears, resembling the previous one.

The difference is that this dialog window only applies to this worksheet. The other window regulates the settings for all Lotus 1-2-3 worksheets.

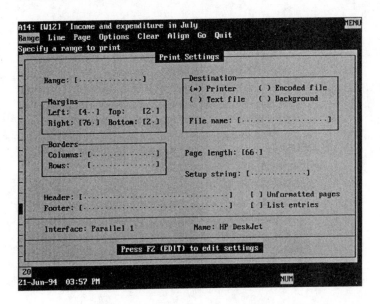

If you want to change the page length for this particular worksheet alone, you have to do that via this dialog window.

The Range section at the top left of this window shows the selected range to be printed. You have to select a range otherwise nothing will be printed.

☞ Select **Range**.
☞ Specify the range you want to print, all the data from June for instance, A1..F11.

When you have confirmed the range by pressing **Enter**, the dialog window appears once more showing the specified range.

If you think that this is a lot of work, first mark the range you want to print and then choose the **Print** menu. Lotus 1-2-3 then presumes that you want to print the marked range.

We have the appropriate specifications for our particular worksheet but if you want to make other settings, select,**Options** from the **Printer** menu. This enables you to make adjustments to the margins, to add headers and footers (sections of text shown at the top and bottom of all pages), to print column and row titles etc.

☞ Select **Go**.

The range will be printed.

☞ Select **Quit** to return to the worksheet.

Printing a worksheet with WYSIWYG format

You also want to print the school report. Not that the marks were all that good, but your grandad is crazy about music and he always gives you a couple of quid if you've done well in this subject at school. Although this is a normal worksheet without a chart, you have to print it in a different way than the worksheet in the previous section. That is because you used the WYSIWYG module. The worksheet has to be printed via that module otherwise the special effects which you have applied using the WYSIWYG module will not appear on paper.

Remove any other worksheets from the screen (**Worksheet, Erase**), and retrieve the REPORT.WK1 worksheet.

☞ Mark the range A1..O23.
☞ Press the : key to open the WYSIWYG menu.
☞ Select **Print**.

An extensive submenu appears along with a dialog
window.

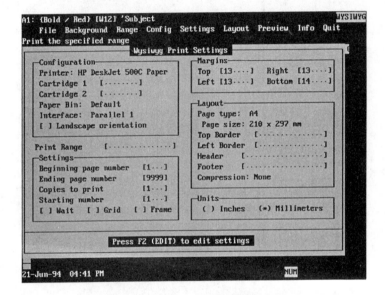

The dialog window is a little different from the dialog window with the default worksheet. In this window, you work with millimetres as the unit of meas-
ure instead of lines and characters, because the
lines no longer have the same size. This is all much
more exact.

The **Settings** and **Layout** submenus contain most of
the options for changing the printer settings.

The **Settings** menu provides options for specifying a page number, the number of copies to be printed, and whether a frame and gridlines should be printed. The **Layout** menu provides options for setting the margins, placing headers and footers, printing column and row titles etc.

The **Compression** option from the **Layout** menu is very useful. It enables you to shrink a wide worksheet so that the entire area fits on to one page. In our case, this is not necessary because our worksheets all fit on one page up until now. But it will undoubtedly occur that you create a worksheet which may be too wide to fit on the page and will therefore require compressing. This is done as follows:

☞ Select **Preview**. This shows how the worksheet will look when printed. In this way you can check whether or not it is too wide.
☞ Press any key to return to the menu.

If the worksheet is too wide, proceed as follows:

☞ Select **Layout**.
☞ Select **Compression**.
☞ Select **Automatic**.

You can of course choose **Manual** and make the adjustments yourself, But if you choose **Automatic**, Lotus 1-2-3 will automatically calculate the best way of fitting the worksheet or specified range of the worksheet on to the page.

☞ Select **Quit**.
☞ Select **Preview**.

You will now see that everything is neatly ordered on one page and you can begin printing.

☞ Select **Go**.

The range is printed on one page.

☞ Select **Quit**.

Another handy feature for not too lengthy worksheets which do not fit onto the page is to print them vertically on the page instead of horizontally. In other words, the length of the page is used for the rows. Lotus 1-2-3 refers to this as **Landscape Orientation**.

If you want to try out this option, press the **:** key to
open the WYSIWYG module and then choose
Print. The Wysiwyg Print Settings dialog window
appears on the screen.

In the Configuration section, you will see the
Landscape orientation option. If you want to activate this, you have to place a cross between the
square brackets. That is done as follows:

☞ Select **Config** from the options along the top of the
   screen.
☞ Select **Orientation**.
☞ Select **Landscape**.

A cross is now placed between the brackets and the
worksheet will now be printed lengthwise instead of
across.

Remove this cross again; we do not need it for our
worksheet.

You will also have to print the CYCLE.WK1 worksheet using the WYSIWYG module. This is because
you have placed the second chart, which you created using this module, in the worksheet. Both the
worksheet and the chart will be printed in one go if
you specify the appropriate range of cells.

Using PrintGraph to print a chart

With your CYCLE.WK1 worksheet, you also saved
the last chart as an independent file with the extension .PIC. This has the benefit that you can print the
chart separately.

Printing the chart independently of the worksheet is done from the screen with the worksheet. It is done using a completely different print program provided by Lotus 1-2-3. This program is called PrintGraph.

Now you have to start up Lotus 1-2-3 in a different way.

☞ Quit Lotus 1-2-3.
☞ Type behind the DOS prompt:

lotus

☞ Press **Enter**.

The following screen appears:

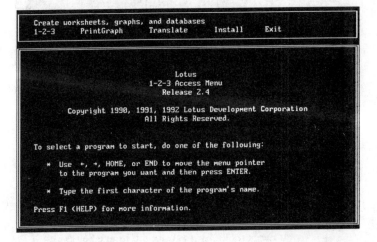

```
Create worksheets, graphs, and databases
1-2-3        PrintGraph      Translate      Install      Exit


                              Lotus
                         1-2-3 Access Menu
                           Release 2.4

          Copyright 1990, 1991, 1992 Lotus Development Corporation
                         All Rights Reserved

To select a program to start, do one of the following:

    * Use +, +, HOME, or END to move the menu pointer
      to the program you want and then press ENTER.

    * Type the first character of the program's name.

Press F1 (HELP) for more information.
```

This is the Lotus opening menu. You can also start up the 1-2-3 program from here. We have not done that up until now because that would have meant an extra and unnecessary step.

The second option on the menu bar is 'PrintGraph'.
Move the cursor to it. An explanatory text appears
above it: 'Print 1-2-3 graph (.PIC) files'. That's exactly what we want.

☞ Press **Enter**.

The PrintGraph main screen appears:

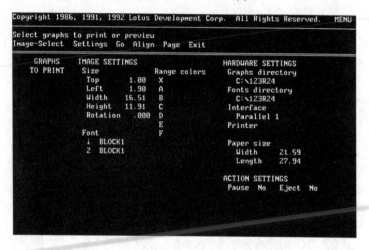

We shall give a brief description of the various
menus so that you will know what to choose later
for your own worksheets.

option   **significance**

Image-Select   By means of the **Image-Select** com-
                     mand, you specify which chart is to be
                     printed or examined.

Settings | As the name indicates, the **Settings** option enables you to specify settings for the charts and for your (hardware) devices. This menu has an extensive submenu: the **Image** option enables you to alter the size of the chart, the fonts for the title and other text. If you have a colour printer, it is also possible to choose colours for the various data ranges in the chart. You can specify the name of your **Printer** under the **Hardware** option.

Go | When you have specified the necessary settings, choose **Go**. This begins the actual printing process.

Align | The **Align** option makes sure that printing will take place at the right place at the top of the paper.

Page | Select the **Page** option to move the paper on so that printing can begin neatly at the top of the next page.

Exit | The **Exit** command returns you to the Lotus opening screen where you can start up Lotus 1-2-3 once more or quit the program completely.

Printing BICYCLE1.PIC

We shall now print the BICYCLE1 chart which you saved as a separate file.

We presume that you still have the PrintGraph program (as shown in the previous figure) on the screen.

You first have to check whether or not your printer
is registered with PrintGraph, otherwise the program will not be able to print because it does not
know which printer is available. If no printer is registered next to 'Printer', proceed as follows:

☞ Select **Settings.**
☞ Select **Hardware**.
☞ Select **Printer**.
☞ Select one of the printers from the list by moving
   the cursor to it and pressing **Enter**.

The name of the printer will appear under 'Printer'.

To avoid having to register the printer each time
you want to use the program, save the new settings:

☞ Select **Quit**.
☞ Select **Save**.

The standard procedure when printing a chart is as
follows. You specify all the necessary settings and
then you specify the name of the chart to be printed. Specifying the chart is done using the **Image-
Select** command.

☞ Select **Image-Select**.

A new screen appears showing the names of all the
charts PrintGraph has found in the specified directory. In our case, that is only BICYCLE1.

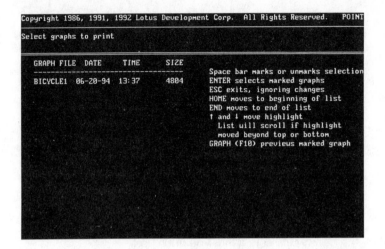

If you want to be absolutely sure that you have chosen the proper chart, press the **F10** key. This places the chart on the screen. Pressing a random key will return you to the screen in which you made the choice of chart.

☞ Press **Enter** to choose the BICYCLE1 chart.

This name will now be shown on screen under 'GRAPHS TO PRINT'.

☞ Select **Go**.

The chart will now be printed. If you now wish to quit the PrintGraph program, choose **Exit**. By choosing **Exit** then **Yes** then **Exit** you will leave Lotus and return to the DOS prompt.

What have you learned in this chapter?

In this chapter we have dealt with printing. As you have seen, that means more than just simply choosing the **Print** option. We shall make a summary of the topics in this chapter:

- printing the standard worksheet
- printing a worksheet via the WYSIWYG module
- printing a chart via the PrintGraph program.

In the next chapter, you will learn how to work with macros, which enable you to quickly and easily execute commands you often use.

Ideas and suggestions

Try printing your worksheets in various sizes or to apply different fonts or font sizes. Don't forget the Landscape Orientation.

Try to make a chart showing the amount of time you have to spend on homework each week. Print it out, photocopy it and spread it among your classmates. You can organize a strike in no time.

7   Making macros

In this last chapter, we shall illustrate how you can simplify your work by defining macros to carry out commands which you often use.

A *macro* is a series of keystrokes which can be executed by simply using one key combination.

If you can master this, you can call yourself a Lotus expert.

Finally we shall show an interesting function that is very convenient if you have to raffle something.

Defining a macro

Before being able to use a macro, you have to define it and also give it a name. This whole process is called *defining*. When you have done this, you can activate the macro as often as you like. This means you have to do a lot of work once, and the rest is a piece of cake.

You type the text for a macro in an empty range in a worksheet. You then give the range a name. This is then the macro name.

The macro name consists of two parts: the backslash (\) and a letter, for example \B. You can then activate the macro by pressing the **Alt** key and then the letter, in this case that would be Alt-B. Of course, you first have to define what the macro has to do.

When typing the commands which the macro has to carry out, you can also type the keys which have special functions. You must type these keys between braces (the curly brackets) so that the program will know that these are special keys and not text. For example, if you want to go to cell A1 in the macro you can use the **Home** key to do this. Then you have to enter this command as {HOME}.

It sounds a little complicated but it is not, as you will see in a moment. First we shall list the most important keys which you can use in a macro and how you should type them if you want to use them.

key	macro registration
Enter	~
↑	{UP} or {U}
↓	{DOWN} or {D}
←	{LEFT} or {L}
→	{RIGHT} or {R}
Home	{HOME}
End	{END}
PgUp	{PGUP}
PgDn	{PGDN}
Go To (F5)	{GOTO}
Backspace	{BACKSPACE} or {BS}
Esc	{ESCAPE} or {ESC}
Del	{DELETE} or {DEL}
slash (to open a menu)	/, < or {MENU}

If you want a complete list, press **F1** for help and press the cursor until you reach Macro Command Index. Then press **Enter**.

Automatic macro

Perhaps you have noticed that when you load a worksheet, the cell pointer is positioned where it was when you saved the worksheet.

This is not always convenient. We shall create a macro which is executed when you load a worksheet and which places the cell pointer in a chosen cell.

This kind of macro is called a self-starting macro and must always be assigned the name \0.

To give an example of this, we shall create a macro
which ensures that whenever you load the
CASH.WK1 worksheet, the cell pointer will automatically be placed in cell B5. This is the first cell in
which data can be entered.

☞ Load the CASH.WK1 worksheet.
☞ Move the cell pointer to cell H1.
☞ Type:

  '\0

☞ Place the cell pointer in cell I1.
☞ Type the following:

  {HOME}{GOTO}B5~

☞ Press **Enter.**

Now you have completed the first part of the macro. In the cell (G1) in front of the actual macro you
have entered the name of the macro to assist your
memory, and in cell I1 you have placed the macro
commands. The {GOTO} command has the same
effect as the **F5** key; it positions the cell pointer in
the chosen cell, in this case B5. The rather strange
character at the end is called a *tilde* and is a macro
command for **Enter.**

We have placed the {HOME} command at the
beginning of the macro so that the whole worksheet will be shown on the screen when the worksheet is displayed. If we did not do this, the chosen
cell, B5, would be placed in the top left-hand corner
of the screen. You would have to move the cell
pointer leftwards yourself to see your data.

We have now arrived at the second part of creating the macro. We must give the range in which it is located a name. Typing the name in the cell in front is not enough; that is only handy for yourself. You must register the name 'officially' with Lotus 1-2-3. This is done in the same way as you normally give a range a name:

☞ Press the / key to open the menu.
☞ Select **Range**.
☞ Select **Name**.
☞ Select **Create**.
☞ Type:

   \0

☞ The instruction 'Enter range:' will appear on the screen. Press **Enter** because the correct range (I1..I1) is already filled in.

The only way to test the macro is to save the worksheet and then load it again.

☞ Press / to open the menu.
☞ Select **File**.
☞ Select **Save**.
☞ Press **Enter** to confirm the name.
☞ Select **Replace**.
☞ Press / to open the menu.
☞ Select **Worksheet** (remember to press **Enter** here - very important!).
☞ Select **Erase**.

The worksheet is now erased from computer memory but is of course stored on disk. Now retrieve it:

☞ Press the / key.
☞ Select **File**.
☞ Select **Retrieve**.
☞ Specify CASH.WK1.

The file is retrieved and the cell pointer is automatically placed in cell B5.

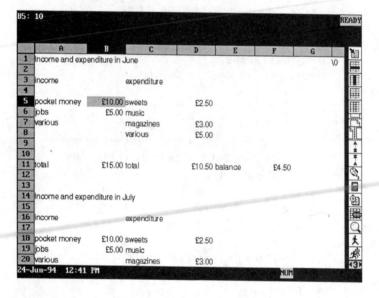

Creating a print macro

Once you have learned how to create macros you will become enthusiastic. It is not difficult to define macros and they do save an awful lot of work. We can imagine that you will want to print your worksheets regularly and it is time-consuming to have to go through all the menus each time.

We shall create a macro to print the June data from your CASH worksheet.

If you are not completely sure of what you should place in your macro, give all the commands necessary to print the file range and write them all down one by one as you go. Don't forget to write down that you have also pressed **Enter**. Defining the macro is then quite straightforward.

To print the June range, the commands are as follows: you press the / key to open the menu, then you press P to open the **Print** menu. Then you press P once more for **Printer**. Then press R for **Range** (you could also press **Enter** here) and specify the range A1..F11 as the range to be printed. This command is concluded by pressing the **Enter** key. Now all the necessary data have been entered and printing can be begun by pressing G for **Go**.

Thus all the macro commands can be placed together as follows:

```
'/PPRA1..F11~G
```

☞ Place the cell pointer in H3 and type:

```
'\P
```

This is to indicate the name of the macro, Alt-P (for printing).

☞ Now go to I3 and type:

```
'/PPRA1..F11~A
```

☞ Press **Enter**.
☞ Press / to open the menu.
☞ Select **Range**.
☞ Select **Name**.
☞ Select **Create**.
☞ Type:

\P

☞ When you have to specify the range, press the
Enter key because the correct range (I3..I3) has
already been filled in.

Check if the macro works by switching on the printer and activating the macro by pressing Alt-P. If
everything has gone as it should, the printer will
begin immediately.

However, you will notice that the paper does not
come out of the printer completely, and Lotus 1-2-3
remains in the print menu. It would be good to
extend the macro a little. We shall add the **Page**
command to our macro and also the **Quit** command to return us to the worksheet screen.

☞ Place the cell pointer in cell I3 once more.
☞ Press **F2** to edit the contents of the cell.
☞ Type:

PQ

☞ Press **Enter**.

Lotus 1-2-3 adopts the new macro into the cell.
Now press the Alt-P key combination again to
check if the print macro now works better.

The section of the worksheet containing the macros now looks like this:

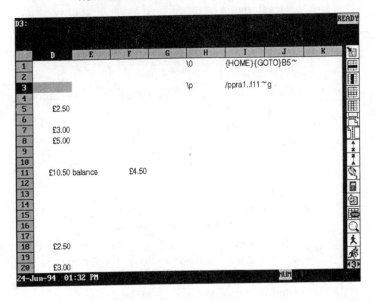

Now save the worksheet and macros.

You have now become familiar with how to apply macros. These are not the most difficult macros but making any macro takes place in exactly the same way.

The @RAND function

Ever had to organize a raffle or a lottery? Or play a game where two sides have to be chosen?

Using Lotus 1-2-3 you can carry out a lottery easily and absolutely fairly. Lotus 1-2-3 has a function

which places a random number between 0 and 1
on the screen. With the knowledge you now have,
you can easily change this to a number between 0
and 10 or 0 and 100.

This function is called @RAND.

Begin a new empty worksheet and type this function in a cell.

☞ Type:

@RAND

☞ Press **Enter**.

The cell now contains a number between 0 and 1,
with six places behind the decimal point. To change
this to a 'normal' number, we have to make some
small adjustments.

☞ Type the following:

@ROUND((@RAND)*10;0)

☞ Press **Enter**.

Now a number between 0 and 10 is shown on the
screen. We have multiplied the number produced
by @RAND by 10. This number has subsequently
been rounded off by means of the @ROUND function to form a whole number.

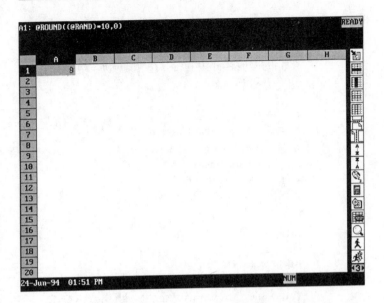

The @ROUND function can be very convenient. It enables you to round off numbers to the nearest whole number; this is convenient for averages which are almost always fractions (see the school report) or for rounding off pence for example. Just as with all functions, the arguments have to be placed between brackets.

To get a new number in the cell, you should press the **F9** key. This key is called the **CALC** key in Lotus 1-2-3. When you press this key, the program recalculates all the formulas in the worksheet again which means in this case that it produces a new random number. If you are playing a game in which two sides have to be picked, you can play odd numbers against even for instance.

What have you learned in this chapter?

We shall make a summary of the topics discussed in this chapter:

- macros
- defining and using macros
  - the self-starting macro
  - the print macro
- the @RAND function
- the @ROUND function
- the CALC key.

Ideas and suggestions

You could save the worksheet with the @RAND function so that you can call up random numbers when you like. You could use these to pick sides for a game or to determine who is to play who in a chess tournament for instance. You could save the results in the same worksheet.

You could make macros to calculate the playing order (perhaps in combination with the @IF function for instance), to calculate the results and to print them. This is not very straightforward but some serious thought and patience will work wonders.

Appendix A
Working with files and directories

In chapter 1, you have learned how to start up Lotus 1-2-3. But it may occur that the program will not start up and the error message 'Bad command or file name' is shown on the screen.

This need not be serious. You may simply have made a typing mistake. Have a close look at the instructions you have typed and try again in any case. If the same message appears again, something has gone wrong.

To find out what this might be, it is necessary to know a little more about files and directories and the way DOS works.

Files and directories

The computer has an internal large disk where files can be stored. These may be program files, such as Lotus 1-2-3 files or WordPerfect files, or may also be files which you have created yourself such as the worksheets you create using Lotus 1-2-3.

This large disk, which we call the *harddisk*, is always referred to as disk C:. Some computers also have other harddisks, D: or E:. This harddisk is divided into *directories*. A directory contains files which

belong together, such as all the worksheets from
Lotus 1-2-3 for instance. The Lotus 1-2-3 program
files are all stored in their own directory and all the
WordPerfect program files are stored together in
another directory.

The Lotus 1-2-3 program directory is probably
called '123R24' in your case.

If you try to start up Lotus 1-2-3, the computer must
know where to find the program files. If you have
not told it where these files are to be found, the
computer will look for them in the current directory,
in other words, in the directory where you are working at the moment (probably C:\).

If you type '123' and the message 'Bad command
or file name appears', this will indicate that the computer cannot find the Lotus 1-2-3 program files in
the current directory. This is probably because they
are located in a different directory. They are probably stored in the '123R24' directory as we mentioned.

You have to change directory to get to them. This is
done by typing the following:

```
cd 123r24
```

This means Change Directory to the 123R24 directory.

Press **Enter**.

The switch is shown on the screen:

```
C:\123R24>
```

It should now be possible to start up Lotus 1-2-3 by typing '123'.

We have not dealt with this topic very deeply, but you should now know enough to start up Lotus 1-2-3.

If you want to know more about files and directories, read the book *Working with DOS and Windows, Be an Expert!* from this series.

Appendix B
List of terms

active cell   The cell where the cell pointer is currently situated in the worksheet. The cell address is always displayed at the top left-hand corner of the worksheet.

address   See *cell address.*

argument   An argument is a part of a *function.* The arguments are the elements to which the function is applied. For instance, the arguments in the @SUM function are the cells which are to be added up.

cell   This is one of the boxes in the worksheet. Each cell is named according to column letter and row number. The first cell in the upper left-hand corner is A1, the very last one in the lower right-hand corner is IV8192.

cell address   The column letter and the row number of a cell, such as A1 for the first cell in the upper left-hand corner of the worksheet.

cell pointer   This is a name for the cursor in the worksheet. The reason is obvious: it always indicates which cell is active.

cursor Behind the *DOS prompt* there is a flashing block or stripe which indicates that the computer is waiting for input from you. This block or stripe is called the *cursor*. In the Lotus 1-2-3 program, this cursor has a different form to indicate the active cell or to select options from the menu.

default This is a term used to indicate the standard settings, in other words, the settings which will apply in the worksheet unless you specify otherwise. For instance, the *default* column width is 9 characters wide.

DOS prompt When you switch on the computer, the *DOS prompt* is shown on the screen. It looks like this:

```
c:\>
```

A flashing *cursor* is shown behind this, which means the computer is waiting on input from you.

extension The part of a file name which is behind the point is the *extension*. This generally indicates the file type. For instance, Lotus 1-2-3 worksheets have the extension .WK1 after the name you have given.

function   A function is a formula which is built into Lotus 1-2-3 and which will calculate something automatically. Each function in Lotus 1-2-3 begins with an *at* sign (@). This enables Lotus 1-2-3 to recognize that you want to use a function and are not entering normal text. Then you specify the name of the function, such as SUM for adding up a number of values. These values, the *arguments*, are placed between brackets.

macro   A macro is a series of keystrokes (representing commands) which can be carried out by pressing one single key combination. This enables you to execute frequently-used commands quickly and easily.

mode indicator   The mode indicator at the top right-hand corner of the screen displays the current state of the program. Normally, the word 'READY' is shown here, which means that Lotus 1-2-3 is ready to accept input. If you press **F2** the word 'EDIT' appears. You can then alter data which have already been entered.

range name   A range name is a name of maximum 15 characters which you have given to a selected range of cells. You can then use the name in formulas and commands instead of having to specify the range of cells, which reduces the chance of (typing) mistakes.

SmartIcons　The icon set flanking the right-hand side of the worksheet is called SmartIcons. Clicking on these enables you to carry out commands quickly and easily if you work with the mouse. You don't have to open the menu bar first.

sort key　A field (column) which is used as the basis for sorting data is called a *sort key*.

status indicator　The statements shown at the bottom of the screen are called *status indicators*. They show what is happening. The statement 'NUM' for example indicates that the **NumLock** key has been pressed.

style　When working in the WYSIWYG mode, you can allocate a name to the formatting settings of a particular cell or range of cells. This is then a *style*. You can apply this style to other cells to give them the same layout.

worksheet　The entire range of rows and columns, thus all cells.

WYSIWYG module　This is the module which you can use to give a more attractive appearance and to print your worksheets and charts.

Index